From Lost to Found
NOWHERE
— NOW HERE —

ANGELÉ MORRIS, MS, LPCC

©2025 by Angelé Morris, MS, LPCC

Published by hope*books
2217 Matthews Township Pkwy
Suite D302
Matthews, NC 28105
www.hopebooks.com

hope*books is a division of hope*media

Printed in the United States of America

First paperback edition.
Paperback ISBN: 979-8-89185-308-9
Hardcover ISBN: 979-8-89185-233-4
Ebook ISBN: 979-8-89185-234-1
Library of Congress Number: 2025938942

Endorsements

Nowhere (now here) is a vulnerable and courageous read. A terrific reminder you are not your trauma, and God is with you through it all. It's not just a story of trauma. Angelé shares biblical and therapeutic knowledge to how she found healing within each page. Further explaining how you can move forward through the journey of hurt and healing. A gentle guide to help you through difficult feelings. Read this book and feel encouraged; you can move forward.

—Lyndi S., MSSW, LMSW

For anyone hurting, broken, or simply trying to navigate their healing journey, this book is for you. Nowhere (now here) is a raw look into the author's story as she leads you through the process of healing, wholeness, and how God values you through trauma. Angelé helps you see God in some of the darkest places, and then helps you navigate to the place God's called you. You will find God on each page and will be blessed and moved by this story of healing.

—Pastor Kenneth Curtis

This book is based on true events. While inspired by real stories, certain details, characters, and events have been adjusted for clarity and to protect privacy. Any resemblance to actual persons, living or deceased, is coincidental. Please be advised that this book walks you through stories of trauma. For guidance tailored to your individual circumstances, please consult a professional for extra information and support. With each chapter, there is a mindfulness practice to ground you and bring a measure of healing. I do not write these stories to trigger you, but to illustrate lost areas. I hope to show you how I became *found and free* so that you can do the same.

Dedication

To God.

To Michael and our children—my greatest earthly gifts.

To my parents, brothers, and spiritual family—thank you for loving me through both the lost and the found.

Table of Contents

Acknowledgements

First and foremost, all glory, praise, and gratitude to God—Father, Son, and Holy Spirit. Thank You for not only bringing me into freedom but also for remaining faithful to Your promise: what the enemy meant for harm, You have used for good.

To my parents—thank you for raising us with God at the center. Your love, your faith, and your courage to break generational cycles of spiritual warfare made room for me to encounter the power of the Holy Spirit in the most beautiful way. You loved me in my lostness and celebrated me in my healing. You never gave up on me, and I'm so grateful for your steadfast prayers and the prayer warriors who stand with you.

To my brothers—your teasing made me resilient, and your love carried me through countless storms and stories. I'm thankful every day for our family bond.

To the love of my life, my husband, Michael—God knew exactly what He was doing when He gave me you. Thank you for walking beside me in my healing journey, for sitting with me in the darkness, and for helping restore what was broken. Your love is a reflection of God's—faithful, safe, and unconditional. I am endlessly grateful for you.

To my son, and to any future children—I see God's light in you. Thank you for your tender hearts, your prayers, and your love for the Lord. I break chains for you, trusting that through God, you will break even more. I count it a sacred honor to raise you from a place of healing, so you can walk in greater freedom.

To my friends and prayer warriors—thank you for embracing all of me, especially the weird and wounded parts. Your love, presence, and support have meant the world to me.

To hope*books Publishing—thank you for believing in me and encouraging me to share the fullness of the story God gave me. Your support and guidance helped bring this book to life, and I am so grateful.

"The Lord has done great things for us, and we are filled with joy."

—Psalm 126:3

CHAPTER 1

Nowhere

"'How do you know me?' Nathanael asked. Jesus answered, 'I could see you under the fig tree before Philip found you.'"

John 1:48

Just as Jesus saw Nathanael under the fig tree, He sees us in our darkest moments, even when we feel unseen.

There is a map, a plan, a process—something that can help your *nowhere* become *now here*.

I walk into my house, body shaking, tears streaming. My only thoughts are getting to my room and hoping no one would know I was home. *How did I get here? How did this happen? Why did this happen? Was it my fault?* As my mind races, my phone vibrates with a text from my mom: "Is that you? Are you home?" I quickly type "yes," but it never sends, so she calls me. I am broken, sobbing, not okay.

I answer because if I don't, then she will be worried. She realizes something is going on by the sound of my voice and tells me to come to her room. I go to her room and as I sob to her, I say words, I hint towards a trauma, but I don't say the words that would make it more real. Because reality just couldn't be true, and this must be a horrible nightmare. He was my friend, and only strangers rape people, or so I believed. I am numb. It is playing in my head, but I can't process it. I remember that as it was occurring, I was able to dissociate and stare at the ceiling. *The Little Mermaid* is what I vaguely remember. I remember the tears. I remember saying "No" many times, and then just giving up. I also remember that when I stopped dissociating and realized again what was happening, I panicked and recall asking if he was wearing protection. He was not wearing any. I remember the words like they happened yesterday as he speaks to me and tells me, "God will forgive you," and quotes scripture over me, but what scripture was quoted, I do not remember.

The devastation I felt flowed over me like a hot lava of knowledge that this is happening, and it must be because I did something wrong. I had to have done something wrong if I am being told God will forgive me. The words played in my head like a nursery rhyme, but instead of comforting me, they mocked me. It would be many years later that I would find out my apology language and understand why I was willing to take responsibility for a trauma. Gary Chapman, author of *The 5 Love Languages,* also wrote *The Five Languages of Apology.* According to this framework, my top apology language is accepting responsibility. Something people with this apology language do through trauma is try to figure out what they did wrong.[1] So, I being blamed added another layer of

---

1   Chapman, Gary D., and Jennifer Thomas. *The Five Languages of Apology: How to Experience Healing in All Your Relationships.* Northfield Pub, 2008.

responsibility, and I lived in a land of questioning what I had done. Plus, someone whom I thought I could trust said those words. Every single seed the Enemy had planted throughout my life sprouted into a garden of death that I then accepted.

I was able to stay in my mother's room that night due to my father being gone. I'm not sure much of what she said, but I recall her comforting me. The fog started to roll in as my brain did its best to protect me from my story. Believing that I was some horrible human being whom God would forgive and unsure as to what I did to deserve what I went through, I was grateful for the fog. I recall someone insulting me months before the occurrence and saying the words, "You're just asking to be raped." At the time, those words were just rude. After the trauma occurred, those words were another lie the Enemy had planted that flourished in the garden of death.

Some of the words I said to my mother were things that had been said to me throughout my life. Lies that had taken hold of my young girl's heart and cultivated soil where all the Enemy had to do was plant the seeds, and they rooted very well into inner dialogue that would haunt me for many years to come. This is where my land of *nowhere* became solidified, but the seeds had been planted long before.

As I wrote this story, I felt tears of compassion for that version of myself. I have tears for your story, too. I am praying for you. I am grateful for making it to where I am today, and I am so excited for you to join me.

So now what? How do I get out of *nowhere*? Lies that occurred throughout my life were spoken to me, around me, or about me. One thing that was never spoken out loud was my sexual abuse by a female friend as a younger girl. I recall being around maybe

NOWHERE (NOW HERE): *From Lost to Found*

seven. It was not discussed, so as a young girl, I just thought that if it were important not to do, people would tell me. Anytime that friend and I hung out, things would occur that I now know were not right, and my heart breaks for not only me, but for my friend too. We were young, innocent, and unaware of what was happening. We never talked about it, never healed together, and I just pray that she is walking in the freedom I now get to walk in.

That experience, though, was an area where the Enemy gathered intel, started to speak his lies over me, and I chose to live with them. The Enemy had it out for me from a young age, and only by the grace of God have all his attempts been thwarted. I am taking what the Devil meant for destruction and letting God make it good. Right now, I claim that victory for you, too. So please know that I am coming to you from the stories of my hurt, so that you can know I understand, but I am also ready and excited to support you in getting one step closer towards freedom. I want you to get from *nowhere* to *now here*, and I am ready to journey with you. To sit in the darkness until you want to be in the light. To cry with you as you heal your child self, and to help you understand the areas where God protected you even through unimaginable trauma. However, through my story and sharing how He protected me, I hope you will also know where your protection was.

This journey is not going to be easy, but I promise it will be worth it. If you need a break as you are reading, I invite you to take that break. In the back of the book is a list of things for you to do if your inner child is struggling. I want you to be able to take the time necessary to walk your inner child towards healing. The child does not need to be rushed, and if you know anything about children, normally, they take longer when they are being rushed. I want to help you cultivate safety for your child self. Jesus tells us to "let the little children come to me" (Matthew 19:14), and that is what I am

- 4 -

inviting you to do. Invite your child self to be loved towards heal-ing. Not only do you deserve to be healed, but your child self does also, and the Bible tells us we get to live an abundant life!

Are you ready to begin the journey? Let's take the first step together!

To find where we are going, we want to know where we are. Let us start in the middle of *nowhere*. *Nowhere* is everything I am, and everywhere I've been—it has encompassed me more than I care to admit. I have wondered if this is a land that is only mine, or if there are others who have felt it. I believe there are many of us in this isolated *nowhere* that we do not know how to explain, and only those who have been here can truly understand the confusion that lies in this land. This journey is one I wish I had not had to travel, and my hope and prayer is that through the information I have received, I can help you get from *nowhere* a lot faster. That way, you can truly learn to love the spaces you are in, even when they are unexplainable.

I always wanted someone to truly understand where I was at and what it was like. I had the blessing of finding it for myself, and now I have the honor of working with people to get to where they want to be emotionally. All the feelings, all the spaces, and the many times you wonder: *Will anyone ever truly know me, and if they end up knowing me, will they like me?* I know Someone who thinks you are to die for, and I am excited for you to go on this journey with me so you can come to the realization that He has already found you. He has always known you, before you were even a thought in your parents' eyes. He has known what your story would look like and has figured out how to make it all good at some point. My good could have been sooner, maybe, but my good is now, and I do not regret the journey I have been on to get here. I do not ask why anymore; I ask God: *What do you want me to do with this?* He wants me to help you, dear reader, get from lost to found.

Let's explore a literal space of *Nowhere.*

I am driving home from college; it is the first time driving home in the snow. I always take the back roads home; they are easy, and I know them. That is, they were easy when the landmarks were not covered in snow. Now I am in the middle of *nowhere,* and I call my dad (this is before phones with GPS or smart cars). "Dad, where am I?!" I ask frantically, and he responds, "I don't know." He cannot tell me; he is not with me. He stays on the phone with me until I get to the correct turn. I had not missed it, and now maybe in the future I will know this road in both the fall and winter seasons. I was lost, and my dad could not fully help me. I was lost and he could not find me. That story occurred about eighteen years ago; however, my story of *nowhere* began as an even younger girl. That was a literal moment of being lost, but my emotional and spiritual *nowhere* felt far more overwhelming.

I have lived in the emotional and metaphorical land of *nowhere* longer than I would like to admit. I dreamed of God granting me my request of a book only for me, a book that, daily, would say something like, "Dear Daughter, today you will face this challenge, and this is how I want you to handle it." I was waiting for a map, an idea about an area so that I could get out of *nowhere* and into somewhere. Everyone else fit somewhere, but even when I was somewhere, I always felt *nowhere.*

Have you ever felt that way? There are others like me, but I feel as if I have not found them in my personal life. If you are intrigued by this space or wondering more, please keep reading. If you are wondering what in the world you borrowed from the library or bought—return the book or give it to someone else, but if you are still reading and are still here, then I say welcome, and I am glad you are here. You are seen and known. God knows exactly where you are, and He wants to get you to your present place.

I did not understand the fullness of God or abundant living. I have now learned that when I feel like I am *nowhere* and I call out to my Heavenly Father and say, "Dad, where am I?"—not only does God calm me down like my earthly father did, but God knows exactly where I am, who I am and whose I am. He sees me, He sees you. Please let that sink in. Sit with that for a moment. You are never so far gone that He is not there, you are never so lost that He cannot find you, and you are never *nowhere* when you are with Him.

I wanted a map back then—a list of what to do and a map of where to go. I still sometimes long for a more descriptive idea of what I am supposed to do, but the closer I walk with God, Jesus, and the Holy Spirit, the more I am naturally doing things supernaturally.

So, where are our maps?

On a hiking trail, you get to the beginning and see the comforting words, "You are here"—that is what I longed for—a clear sign of my location and direction. No sign has ever told me what I have felt: that I am *Nowhere* and there's no way out. Life doesn't offer a map or a clear sign of where to go next. Unlike the comforting "You are here" markers in malls, I often felt there was no way out of my "*nowhere*." Life does not seem so clearly laid out, so wonderfully mapped, or planned. I did not know how to find it. I believe I was meant to create it, through my story, so that hopefully others may find what they need through my journey. I find it interesting that I am often geographically lost, and this deeply relates to my emotional and spiritual world.

So, WHERE DO YOU BEGIN WHEN YOU ARE IN THE MIDDLE OF *NOWHERE?*

I started where I was and have been on that journey ever since. I want to journey with you, dear reader, and hopefully some of what God has shown me will be exactly what you need to know and hear to become found.

In our last chapter, we will see how our *nowhere* truly goes into the *now here,* but right now, we start where we are.

MINDFULNESS PRACTICE: WALKING IN THE GARDEN OF YOUR SOUL

1. Pause and Acknowledge the Present

Wherever you are—reading or listening to this book, lying on your bed, sitting on your couch, or on the move—take a moment to pause.

- Place your hand on your heart.
- Take a deep breath in through your nose and exhale through your mouth with a big sigh.
- Feel your heartbeat. That rhythm is where you are right now.

2. Ground Yourself in Love

Breathe again. Let it sink in: *You are known, you are seen, and you are loved.* Allow this truth to swirl through your thoughts and settle into your soul.

3. Journey in Thought or Action

If you're able to move, take a short walk. If not, walk with me in your thoughts. Imagine yourself stepping into the **Garden of Your Soul**—a beautiful, peaceful space where God is walking with you.

4. Explore the Garden

- Picture vibrant flowers and lush scenery, symbols of beauty and growth.
- Notice weeds and thorny overgrowth—areas representing pain, struggles, or unresolved emotions.

5. Invite God's Presence

Look at God with the questions and emotions that arise. In your imagination, see His love for you in His eyes as He gently asks, *"Do you want to start pruning?"*

- Allow yourself to say "yes" to His work.

- Take another deep breath. Imagine God's hands working alongside you, removing what is not from Him.

6. Let Emotions Rise

If you feel emotions welling up, let them come. If tears fall, know they are not wasted—they are the fertilizer of your soul's garden.

7. Reflect on Transformation

Recall that pruning, weeding, and tilling the soil are painful but necessary. Healing holds a purpose, even when the process feels hard. The Bible promises that he makes all things new (Revelation 21:5), and your soul's garden is no exception.

8. Closing Thought

- Remember this: your tears are precious to God, your heart is known to Him, and your healing is His delight.

- End with a prayer or moment of gratitude for the Master Gardener's work in your soul.

As we move into the next chapter, thank you for walking this journey with me. Take time to process, knowing that each step forward is a step closer to healing.

CHAPTER 2

What are You Wearing?

Getting ready that night was so much fun. A few of my friends and I had made plans that for the theme bowling night, we would go from the era of the 1950s dressed in poodle skirts. We had gone together to rent the skirts for the evening. I was so excited, as I had always wanted to wear a poodle skirt. I dressed in care and made sure that I showed modesty. The outfit was simple but beautiful. My friends and I had a lot of fun, and the pictures give the memories of who I was before my assault occurred. My guy friend was unable to come, so after the event, he stated he had wanted to see my outfit. It was supposed to be fun and innocent. Too often, we hear the statement that "women/girls are asking for it" by what they are wearing. The day after bowling and my assault, I went to my internship with swollen eyes—I told them it was allergies. I had homework/lunch plans with another friend, and when I told him what had happened, he asked what I was wearing. The Enemy used that conversation to add to my narrative of "this is my fault." I took so much care getting dressed that night, but I was not dressed spiritually. The lies were able to take root in my soul.

BEING CLOTHED IN RIGHTEOUSNESS—ISAIAH 61:10, NLT

As we journey together from *nowhere* to *now here*, I want to make sure you're spiritually protected, and with that comes exploring: what are you wearing?

Every single day, we get dressed or change clothes. Something God brought to my attention is that many Christians are not spiritually dressed. Or they are dressed—but in their own clothing and armor and nothing from the Father, Son, and Spirit. For a while, I was neither; I never fully understood it nor how to do it. I mean, do not get me wrong, I prayed—and I prayed a lot—but it was not working, and it just made me feel like I was continuing to fail. I would pray the scriptures "be anxious for nothing" (Philippians 4:6) and "God hath not given us the spirit of fear" (2 Timothy 1:7, KJV), yet I was wearing clothes the Enemy gave to me with anxiety or fear as their labels.

In the mental health therapy world, we have different modalities; when I started my training in Psychosomatic therapy and emotionally focused therapy, I realized some important things that we can do in our faith to help us. By "us," I mean those of us who, for some reason, need a unique modality that helps us to not only know the truth but to feel it. Other people can just logically see what Scripture says and no longer live in fear. I needed something different due to my story and the way Satan started coming after me when I was young, bringing with him fearful things.

While I was still in my parents' household, they prayed the armor of God over me often. When I left, I was not praying that for myself, and so unbeknownst to me, the armor I was then allowing myself to wear was from Satan. The lies began before anything bad really occurred. As a young girl, I would hear voices in my head—they were loud and brought upon my young body an anxiety I would carry deep in my soul, unaware of it because it had become a part of me. If I did not have godly parents aware of spiritual warfare, I believe I may have been put into a hospital when I told my parents. Instead, their prayers changed for me, and the protection was different. I then began experiencing seizures, which were a spiritual space that cultivated so many stories of *nowhere*, and so many stories of chaos that I will address in more detail in future chapters. The doctors could not figure it out, but my parents did. As a young child, when those kinds of things start to occur, the Enemy gets to whisper to your soul stories that have not unfolded, but are preparation for his attempts to thwart God's plans for your life.

I had friends, but those friends betrayed me, lied to me, and called me names, either to my face or behind my back. I had two older brothers who would tease me, but I was more fragile inside than anyone was aware. So, the story of who the Enemy said I was began, the words that flowed over me were: ugly, unwanted, not a part, invisible, unworthy, no good, nothing, no one, lost, weird, nerd, and *nowhere*. So, the mask wearing started at an age I'm not even fully aware of, because what child doesn't start wearing some type of mask? The masks that became more detrimental to my story started around ten. I so wanted to be liked, so I pretended not to care. I teased myself more than others could, so that it seemed it didn't faze me. The story of intimacies started then, too. *We were friends, we were only playing house, so it was fine, right?* But it led to things that started to cultivate more of a darkness that I couldn't talk about. *So now I'm impure, and that is bad according to the church. So be quiet and don't talk.*

When I was fourteen, although I was not allowed to date until I was sixteen, a boy told me that if I didn't date him, he would commit suicide. *Now the feelings of other people's stories are my responsibility, and things are my fault.* It's what he said. The stories continue, one major story of sexual grooming, and other minor stories. The enemy continued to plant. The lies continued to swirl. My identity was in what the world said or what I could find to anchor to. The problem with the anchors of this world is that they are just a figment of our imagination, and they are constantly moving, pulling us under instead of keeping us steady.

Then I was twenty-two years old, innocent, naive, and oh, did I want to be wanted and loved. The assault occurred, and I experienced a waterfall effect of the past twenty-two years of the Enemy's story upon my life, and I believed everything was solidified. I spiraled for quite a few years on a dark slide that was forever twisting to a new moment, the Enemy reminded me who he said I was. Every time I thought I hit the bottom of my darkness and the depths of despair, the slide would curve, and I would go deeper into the darkness.

As I was writing this book, God gave me the chapter names before I was fully aware of all He wanted me to write. It was not until our publisher Brian Dixon encouraged us authors that if we felt stuck with our writing, we may need to look at what we were holding onto. I told him and my cohort that at first, I thought my book would be mini testimonies with exercises and guides, but then I realized my book needed to be more of me. After Brian read my comment aloud, he responded, "Your book needs to be all of you, my friend." Tears welled in my eyes, knowing it would be harder to write, giving my all to it.

When I looked at my outline again, I burst into tears reading this chapter's title because I finally realized what it meant. It can't just be the armor of God; it must be tied to the question I was asked, the lies I believed, and how spiritually He protected me, but I was also spiritually not dressed. It sometimes takes years to understand how God can take the bad and make it beautiful or make it make sense.

It took years for me to understand how He protected me, because allowing an assault to occur in your life or sexual abuse to occur as a child does not sound like protecting. God gave me a vision at the end of 2024 that before the assault ever occurred, He hid the little girl me in the shelter of His wings. In that vision, He lovingly brought her to me, and now all of me is connected. I am now able to have faith like a child again. I encourage you to "have faith like a child." I encourage you to invite that little child to where you are now and start journeying with her or him towards healing.

During the assault, He created my brain in such a beautiful way that it dissociated, so that I didn't have to be fully present. He allowed a fog to roll in because I didn't know what to do and was not ready for healing. He got me to my internship the next day, and with swollen eyes, I worked. I didn't want to alarm anyone the day after because I wanted to just do my job, so I stated it was allergies. Unfortunately, when I cry, I tend to cry so passionately that I get swollen eyes. He did not author the sin upon my life, but He is the author of my brain, and the author of how it was able to protect me.

I'm now a mental health therapist, and when life has brought a struggle that has caused me to cry, I would show up to work, but I would still state it was allergies that caused my swollen eyes. I am sorry for where the lie began, and I am sorry that it is one I choose to carry to protect others. I am just grateful for the tears now—they are fertilizer for my soul's garden. I am also grateful for the authentic space I choose to live in—now I will be honest with anyone if it is true allergies, or if life is giving me some difficult moments. Because although I have been a mental health therapist for ten years, I am still a human being, and life still occurs in my personal world.

WHAT ARE YOU WEARING?

Now, I want to explore with you, and I want you to hear it from someone who was asked this question right after trauma and who cares about your soul: What are you wearing? What are the clothes you have on? Not your literal clothes, but what are you wearing spiritually? Did you know that you can wear the armor of God every day, that it is a practice we get to do, and that the Holy Spirit gets to protect us?

Something I tell my clients is that just because you have done the salvation prayer, does not mean you are wearing the helmet of salvation. The Bible tells us we should put on our helmet of salvation, and I believe we should be doing this daily. I have worn my own helmet way too often and my own breastplate of righteousness. My breastplate of righteousness, I knew, was not from God, but I never fully understood the belt of truth. Priscilla Shirer's *The Armor of God* videos and workbook truly helped me to understand the belt of truth. It is the Bible; it is God's truth and what God says.[2] God has helped me to see that the belt of truth is like a charging port for the other items; it not only holds the breastplate of righteousness up so it is not too heavy, but it can hold the sword of the Spirit and the shield of faith. I am starting to realize that my faith may be smaller than a mustard seed, but I know that God's faith is bigger, and I keep asking Him to give me His shield of faith to see Him in the valley of the shadow and on the mountain tops.

---

2 Shirer, Priscilla. *The Armor of God Video Series.* LifeWay Press, 2015.

Armor of God

So let us open our Bibles and look at Ephesians to understand what we are meant to be wearing. Ephesians 6:10–18 (NLT) gives us guidance in what we are meant to wear and do.

A final word: Be strong in the Lord and in his mighty power. Put on all of God's armor so that you will be able to stand firm against all strategies of the devil. For we are not fighting against flesh-and-blood enemies, but against evil rulers and authorities of the unseen world, against mighty powers in this dark world, and against evil spirits in heavenly places. Therefore, put on every piece of God's armor so you will be able to resist the enemy in the time of evil. Then after the battle you will still be standing firm. Stand your ground, putting on the belt of truth and the body armor of God's righteousness. For shoes, put on the peace that comes from the Good News so that you will be fully prepared. In addition to all of these, hold up the shield of faith to stop the fiery arrows of the devil. Put on salvation as your helmet, and take the sword of the Spirit, which is the word of God. Pray in the spirit at all times and on every occasion. Stay alert and be persistent in your prayers for all believers everywhere.

Wow. Read that again. I cannot tell you how many times I have read that, and even now, as I typed it into this book, new things stood out. Let us break this down.

First, we need to be strong in the Lord and His mighty power—it does not say be strong in self and our own strength, but be strong in the Lord and His mighty power. Second, we need to put on the armor so that we can stand firm against all strategies of the devil. It does not say that the Enemy will not attack us or that we will not feel anything—we put it on so that we can stand. Third, it is a good reminder that we are not fighting each other. Please, I pray you understand this, ask God to give your eyes supernatural power to see in the spiritual realms so that we will stop fighting and judging one another.

Now the scripture tells us to put on the armor—okay, why? So that after the battle we can still stand firm. Notice again it does not say we will not have battles; it does not say we will win the battles—it says we will be standing firm. Firm in our salvation, firm in truth, firm in peace, and firm in God. Thank you, Jesus!

As we read verse fourteen, we get into what we are meant to wear. Put on the belt of truth and the body armor of God's righteousness. Thank you, Jesus, for the truth of the gospel. Thank you, Jesus, that it is your righteousness because we are unworthy and unrighteous. Thank you that Jesus took our place. Next, we put on the shoes that are the peace that comes from the good news. It is not saying that it is the peace of our circumstances or that we are always in peace. It reminds us to know what the Bible says so that we can stand firm in the peace of His good news. "Hold up the shield of faith to stop the fiery arrows of the devil" (Ephesians 6:16, NLT). Hold up—not create, not make, not figure out, not have enough—Hold up what God has already given you, HIS faith. I just need to sit here myself with this one. I have always tried to have enough faith, faith as small as a mustard seed, and I just could not. I have faith in God, and that has helped my faith to grow immensely because I am continually asking for His eyes to see and His faith to move. Verse seventeen says, "Put on salvation as your helmet, and take the sword of the Spirit, which is the word of God." Again, this is not saying "Oh, you are saved, so you are good." Priscilla Shirer references it as *applying* your salvation.[3] We

---

3 Shirer, Priscilla. *The Armor of God Video Series.* LifeWay Press, 2015.

must put on our salvation so that we are in the correct army. The last verse from this section tells us to "pray in the Spirit at all times and on every occasion." I am not a Bible scholar, so I will only give my views on this for those of you from a Pentecostal/Evangelical background—you don't need to only pray in tongues. The Holy Spirit is with us and within us right now, guiding us. When I am often unsure what to do or how to pray, I often say, "Holy Spirit, please give me clarity and wisdom and insight, walk with me and guide me." I also know that Jesus, in this moment, is sitting on the right side of God intervening on our behalf. Right now, I am praying they are all three sitting with you as you learn how to let them give you the armor meant for you.

When I was *nowhere*, I was not dressed spiritually, and I truly did not know God or myself. It took first finding God, then me, to learn how to get spiritually dressed. The armor has been my constant protection; my greatest support. I jokingly tell people that I have a pajama set of armor, too, and that I never take it off unless God wants to restore a piece.

I think something major for whoever is reading this right now to know is that you may think you are *nowhere* and lost to others or yourself, but God sees you, knows you, loves you, and has called you to Him.

Before we get to this exercise, I want to say thank you for choosing to show up at this place, to do the work. I wish I could do emotionally focused therapy with everyone of you to help you walk through this, and so right now I am praying for you. As you step into this spiritual space of putting on your armor, I pray that your mind will be renewed, that clarity and focus will reign. If this is too hard right now, put a bookmark in this spot and just breathe. Mark this chapter so you can come and visit this place of spiritual protection.

MINDFULNESS PRACTICE: PUTTING ON THE ARMOR OF GOD

Introduction

Find a quiet, comfortable space. Sit down, close your eyes, and focus on your breathing. Take a deep breath in through your nose, and exhale through your mouth with a big sigh. Do this a few more times until you feel centered.

Pray with me:

"Father God, Jesus, and Holy Spirit, I invite You into this moment. Show me if I am wearing Your armor, my own armor, or if I am unprotected. Help me to surrender what is not from You and fully clothe myself in Your truth and power. Amen."

1. The Belt of Truth

- Place your hands near your waist.

- Reflect: *Am I living in God's truth, my own truth, or confusion?*

- Pray: *"Lord, I surrender my own version of truth. Wrap me in Your belt of truth so I can stand firm in You."*

- Imagine fastening the belt securely, feeling its strength around you.

2. The Breastplate of Righteousness

- Place your hands over your heart.

- Reflect: *Am I relying on my own righteousness, or am I covered by God's righteousness?*

- Pray: *"Lord, guard my heart with Your righteousness. Protect me from pride and self-reliance."*

- Imagine placing the breastplate over your chest, feeling its protection.

3. The Shoes of Peace

- Wiggle your toes or imagine slipping on sturdy shoes.
- Reflect: *Am I walking in God's peace, my own strength, or chaos?*
- Pray: *"Lord, guide my steps. Help me walk in peace and share Your good news with others."*
- Visualize lacing up the shoes and standing firmly.

4. The Shield of Faith

- Imagine holding a shield in front of you.
- Reflect: *Is my faith in God strong, wavering, or misplaced?*
- Pray: *"Lord, strengthen my faith. Help me trust You to extinguish the Enemy's fiery arrows."*
- Picture the shield growing stronger in your hands, deflecting attacks.

5. The Helmet of Salvation

- Place your hands on your head.
- Reflect: *Am I confident in my salvation, or am I struggling with doubt?*
- Pray: *"Lord, protect my mind with the assurance of salvation. Help me think thoughts that align with Your truth."*
- Visualize placing the helmet securely on your head, guarding your thoughts.

6. The Sword of the Spirit

- Extend your hand as if holding a sword.

- Reflect: *Am I wielding the Word of God effectively, or am I unarmed?*

- Pray: *"Lord, equip me with Your Word. Teach me to speak and act boldly in Your truth."*

- Picture the sword in your hand, gleaming with power and authority.

CLOSING PRAYER

Now, imagine yourself fully clothed in the armor of God. Stand tall, feeling protected and empowered. Pray:

"Lord, thank You for equipping me with Your armor. Help me walk in faith and truth, ready to stand firm in You. Amen."

Congratulations! Now you are fully clothed in the armor of God! The best clothing you can ever wear. I am so proud of you for doing this practice and walking through it to make sure that you are dressed appropriately as a Christian. This is one step closer from being lost to found.

CHAPTER 3
Holy Spirit Backdraft

Excitement courses through my body. I am fifteen years old and—finally—not only do I get to drive out of town, but I get to drive to my friend's for a sleepover! As I'm driving there, listening to music, I am preparing for a chill night—music, movies, laughter.

The night unfolded in a way that felt like it could only happen in a movie. It was just supposed to be the two of us, but she had invited other friends over. They were girls I did not know. The night started out okay until someone pulled out a satanic board game. No way was I going to participate in that! Sure, I had done things with this friend that my parents weren't aware of, but those were overall innocent. This was an area I was not even going to try. I went into the friend's room, grabbed a Bible, opened it, and started reading. Time for me was unknown during this event in my teen years. All I recall is them rushing into the room yelling, "Angelé, Help us!" My brain did a quick scramble, and I started to pray. The presence of something grew stronger, and my chest tightened.

I grabbed the Bible and I kept praying. I started walking back and forth, only to run into an invisible wall that knocked me down. Fear was trying to grasp at me, the fear I've known throughout my childhood, but a deeper fear that was more real than just my imagination. I got up and continued to pray, bind, and rebuke. I closed spiritual doorways that the girls must have opened. The pressure was getting more intense, my heart was racing, and I was doing everything I knew to do. I looked into the vanity mirror only to see a demonic face looking back at me. I bound that. The chaos stopped, the storm calmed, and the girls were okay. I was okay literally, but spiritually, I was shaken.

I would like to tell you that I lived in the victory that was won that day, but unfortunately, the teen brain chose to live in fear, and that was the day I shut myself off to the spiritual world. The lie I believed was that the fear was stronger than the victory, that I truly did not accomplish anything in this moment. The Enemy again came with a truth wrapped in a lie. I did not win the victory in this story, but the Holy Spirit won the victory because I was able and willing to fight spiritually. I didn't realize that by shutting myself off to the Enemy spiritually, I would also close the door to the Holy Spirit, to the power that always will win and allows me spiritual victory. I didn't tell people about that story even though I thought I did. It was just another story I kept inside myself, locked away.

WHERE'S THE HOLY SPIRIT?

As we have learned to navigate the beginning spaces of *nowhere*, and we are now dressed in the armor of God, we can step into knowing the fullness of the power of the Holy Spirit. The Holy Spirit is often depicted as a dove or flame, but His power is far greater than these symbols. He is part of the Trinity, actively working in our lives to guide and protect us. Let me share how He revealed this to me in a moment when I felt *nowhere* once again.

In 2019, I was many years past the assault. I was navigating different hurts and pains of my story, and it was my first year of marriage. Even if you've done healing work, marriage comes with a different level of healing and understanding yourself. I went for a drive to see my husband, where he was working about two hours away. As I was driving, I started to see the flare (pump jack flare) from an oil field rig pad—it was dark, and I could see one flare, then a little way further, I could see another. In that moment, God showed me how the Holy Spirit flares are waiting to fire back at the Enemy, and the Holy Spirit is waiting for us to ask.

The Bible tells us that we are in victory (Revelation 3:21–22) and that God has already gone before us in our story (Deuteronomy 31:8). He showed me how the Holy Spirit's flares are strategically placed on my path for everything that will occur in this life. As I am witnessing what God is showing me and giving me imagery for, I get hit with the beauty of His power and the power of His love. I had started to feel like I was *nowhere* again. I was praying to get to who God wanted me to be, and partially wishing that I could go back to who I used to be, before anything traumatic had ever occurred. But in that moment, in that space, I saw how to move forward on this journey and that the Holy Spirit is ready and waiting with fire to fight back when the Enemy tries to shoot arrows or flames at me. So, when I know I am in a battle and the story feels real, I can give the Holy Spirit permission to fight even more, and He can utilize that flame He has put there strategically to cause a backdraft on the Enemy and create havoc for him.

A backdraft is a term utilized in the firefighting industry. A backdraft occurs when oxygen ignites a fire that has been starved. In the same way, the Holy Spirit's power is ready to ignite against the Enemy when we invite Him in, breathing spiritual life into our battles. When we are in a battle, we need to bring life and oxygen to the Holy Spirit's power so that the backdraft can work. That's why it is important to praise in the storm, take action in faith, and thank Him for a breakthrough that may not have occurred yet. When we are in a story, we forget to breathe in God's breath and sometimes lean on our own understanding or strengths. When we breathe in God's breath, we are getting oxygen to the Holy Spirit so He can fight on our behalf. We are remembering that Jesus has already won.

I wish I had seen this sooner for my story, but I can see the areas where, unbeknownst to me, it was happening, and it was there. Not only has God shown me this, but He has also opened my eyes to how evident His presence is in the midst of chaos or suffering. It is written in Psalm 23, which many people have memorized, but we can all benefit by truly meditating on it, that He prepares a table for us in the presence of our enemies. Not only was I not utilizing the Holy Spirit fire while going through things, I also was not sitting down at my table and eating the bountiful, restorative food God has given to all of us. I kept waiting for the perfect opportunity to get out of the shadow of darkness. Instead, I have learned how to sit at the table and let the Holy Spirit's fruit be my meal. It has been such a wonderful blessing to sit down and rest, knowing that God has my story and my life.

A backdraft needs specific conditions: a fire starved of oxygen and a sudden breath of air. Similarly, the Holy Spirit's power ignites when we invite Him into our struggles. By believing He will, the Enemy is thwarted. Instead of the Enemy's fiery arrows hitting you, the Holy Spirit will backdraft him, and the arrows will fall in defeat. The Enemy will always fall in defeat because Jesus has already won.

The imagery that night on the road was powerful for me, and

if you do not know what an oil rig flare looks like in North Dakota, feel free to look it up. While I was driving up every hill, around every bend, there was a new flare for me to see, as God spoke to me not only through that imagery but also through songs.

Those songs that played were "Mistakes" by Influence Music and "The Rock Won't Move" by Vertical Worship.

I truly want you to know you are not here by mistake, that you are not a mistake, and that you can be free and found. The lyrics of the song "Mistakes" spoke over me in ways I wasn't aware I needed. It identifies how God doesn't make mistakes, and so because of that, I am not a mistake.[4]

I started to cry as the song "Mistakes" played out. As I focused on the words, I realized I was living in the lie of "I must be a mistake," especially with who I am, who I'm becoming, and what I have gone through. Have you ever felt this way? Like a mistake? If so, I see you, I understand, and although I read the scriptures of being beautifully and wonderfully made, it took this song, this beat, to truly help my heart to understand (Psalm 139:14).

As I was sitting in God's presence, the next song, "The Rock Won't Move," started to play. The lyrics of the song washed over me, and I started to cry again because the rock *has* moved in my life, and it has not stayed true.[5] God then showed me the imagery of me on the rock, only it wasn't me on His rock. I had made myself my own rock, and I kept rolling off of His rock because I was still trying to protect myself. As I allowed myself to break down on that car ride, I realized God has always been true; He has stayed constant. Because of my traumas, even though I had put myself on the rock, I hadn't allowed Him fully into all of me. I kept break-

---

4 Influence Music. *Mistakes*. Featuring Melody Noel, Influence Music, 2018.

5 Vertical Worship. *The Rock Won't Move*. Essential Worship, 2013.

ing on this car ride, and now I am on the Rock, as a broken, soft, humbled version of myself who knows that the actual Rock will not move.

What I love about this drive is that through the Holy Spirit, God transformed my journey from *nowhere* to *now here*. He took the ashes of my past and breathed life into them, igniting a flame of hope and freedom. He wants to do the same for you. He has flares waiting to be ignited in your story, waiting for your prayer of praise to bring oxygen to them so that the Holy Spirit can do what only He can do, which is win the war against the Enemy.

As we step into this next practice, allow yourself the beauty of knowing you are perfectly and wonderfully made. Allow yourself to breathe in this space in the knowledge of acceptance for who you are because of what Jesus has done.

MINDFULNESS PRACTICE:
IGNITING THE FLAME WITHIN

Preparation:

- Find a quiet space where you won't be disturbed.

- Bring a journal or piece of paper if you'd like to reflect afterward.

Step 1: Breathing and Centering

- Sit comfortably, close your eyes, and place your hand on your heart.

- Take a deep breath through your nose, hold it for a moment, and slowly exhale through your mouth. Repeat this three times.

- As you breathe, visualize the Holy Spirit's flame within you, steady and waiting.

Step 2: Visualizing the Holy Spirit's Presence

- Picture yourself standing in a dark space. Around you are faint glimmers of light—these are the flares of the Holy Spirit, strategically placed to guide and protect you.

- As you take another deep breath, imagine those flares igniting one by one, lighting your path.

- Whisper this prayer: *"Holy Spirit, ignite the flame within me. Fight for me, guide me, and lead me to victory."*

Step 3: Reflection and Surrender

- Reflect on an area of your life where you feel under attack or overwhelmed.

- Imagine offering this situation to the Holy Spirit, as if

placing it into the flames. Watch as the fire consumes it, turning it into light and strength.

- Take another deep breath and say: *"Holy Spirit, I surrender this battle to You. I trust in Your power and love."*

Step 4: Anchoring in Scripture

- Repeat Psalm 23:5 to yourself: *"You prepare a table before me in the presence of my enemies. You anoint my head with oil; my cup overflows."*

- Visualize sitting at the table God has prepared for you, nourished and safe, even as the Holy Spirit fights for you.

Step 5: Gratitude

- End by thanking the Holy Spirit for His presence, protection, and guidance.

- Write down any thoughts or revelations that came to you during this practice.

CHAPTER 4

How to Breathe

The movement was felt and known by me before it was ever seen. At a very young age, I would try to describe to my parents how, at night, I would experience this unbelievable shaking, and that I couldn't stop. It was not until the winter of 1998 that it was finally witnessed by one of my brothers. The ambulance was called, and we went down a path of figuring out what was wrong. The worst part for me was the inability to function, the inability to breathe, and feeling as if I were in a dungeon within my own body. I recall hearing my parents' voices and trying so hard to get out of whatever this was. The fear inside of me was stronger than any fear I'd ever faced at that point. The muffled voices of those who loved me, trying to get through. The inability to control what is normally controllable. This was the first time my body betraying me was witnessed by others. This is when the fear became more deeply rooted. The voice of the Enemy was scary, but this was not just a voice—this was a prison that was external. As a child and as a young adult, I was breathing because I was alive; it was not an area I was mindful of. It wasn't until my late twenties and early thirties that I learned how to breathe God's breath.

BREATHING GOD'S BREATH

In Genesis 2:7 it says, "Then the Lord God formed a man from the dust of the ground and breathed into his nostrils the breath of life, and the man became a living being." I find it interesting that in the first book of the Bible, we have scripture on the Breath of God, who He breathed the breath of life into humans. I do not feel like I have heard enough about this throughout my life, and I wish I had. It was not until I learned how to breathe like Jesus that I felt like I was able to stop and catch my breath.

I believe that as a young child, I was always in my head, whether writing stories or creating worst-case scenarios. I replayed days, I played days in advance. A lot of times my predictions would come true and therefore I started to live even more in the anxiety of it all as I navigated different things.

Living in my head came with the concept of seizures—I was having them way before I was seen having them. I knew something was not okay. I can remember the fear that would start to come over me—I would wake up and just know something was going to happen before I started shaking uncontrollably and waited to see if I would be able to function again. There is something that comes with the knowledge that your body is no longer yours to control and is being controlled by itself. Mine was filled spiritually, but not in a good way. It was filled with a darkness that cannot be fully explained except to someone who has been in this type of out-of-control space. Seizures were just another way the Enemy had me trapped and controlled in fear.

The first seizure that my family saw, the doctors called a grand mal seizure, and that led to many doctor's appointments and many uncertainties as to what was wrong with me as a child. My body showed all the seizures I had had; I still have seizure marks that are upon my body. They put a blue light against my skin in the darkness, and I had so many seizure spots. So, I was not confused by the shaking of the nights, the randomness I would feel afterwards, or the exhaustion that came; my body showed it was all true. However, the doctors were still unaware of what was causing this to happen to me.

My first known seizure was probably the scariest for me. It was the year 1998, and I was only 10 years old. I know the year, and I know it was December because someone had bought me a Christmas moose that had the year on its foot. I remember snuggling with that moose in the comfort of my parents' bedroom as my young life seemed to be controlled by something that was not me. I recall being in a seizure, and I could hear the voices of my parents saying my name, but for the life of me, I could not respond or get out of this uncontrollable shaking. I felt like I was going to die; I felt like there was a huge weight upon my chest and that I would never come out.

That was the first one anyone saw, and there were more to come as fear became my companion, and breath was just something I did only because I was alive. To hear their voices, to hear my name, and to be unable to respond or get out of it. To be so stuck. I believe parts of this experience are what help me sit longer with people in pain. You can't force someone out of something that is weighing them down. I've been in both the literal and emotional space of the inability to get out, and certain catchphrases in our church did not help. The other seizures were known to me, and scary, but this was the first time I knew how long I was in it, and to know there was support and love on the other side of it, but I was unsure how to get there. They continued to call my name; the voices of those who loved me were praying for me, and they were speaking to me. They were the voices that brought me to freedom. However, at even earlier ages, there were voices that had me trapped.

I want to go back a little further before we move forward. At a young age, I started to hear voices—I did not tell people about them. I believed most people had this because it was my normal, and if others were not talking about it, well then, why would I? I did not always understand them; it just seemed loud and chaotic in my head. I remember one time a group of us were playing hide and seek in our town, and I was by the tree to count, and my head was so loud with two voices arguing with one another. I questioned myself: *Was this just my subconscious speaking to me? But why was there more than one? Oh well, this must be the way brains work.* I went back to trying to focus on the game at hand. The voices spoke lies over me throughout my life. There were moments of freedom, and moments they were quiet, but moments they sparked into attempting to tell me who I was.

Do you remember what it was like to be a child? If no one talks to us about something, we just believe that it is normal. Why would my parents think to talk to me about voices in my head? Yes, that is a random conversation to have with your four-year-old. Few people have it. I have it more commonly than most people due to my profession—you would be surprised to know the amount of people who have heard or are hearing voices and still doing well. People believe that if you hear voices, you will end up in an insane asylum. However, you would also be surprised to know how much of it is more spiritually based. There is a way of determining if it is physical or spiritual, and you can do that with the support of godly counselors and doctors' reports.

Now, back to the first witnessed grand mal seizure in 1998. I was 10 years old, and this was the same year I had a conversation with my parents about how my friends would always come to talk to me because I was trustworthy, and maybe I should find a job like that. That is when I first learned about counseling, and God called me into that career. The path was something that the Enemy did not want me on. The doctors weren't fully sure what was happening and didn't diagnose me with epilepsy, but they recommended medication. My parents, leaning on their awareness of God and the reality of spiritual warfare, sought Him for wisdom. In that process, God led my mom to pay closer attention to my daily habits and begin researching possible triggers. My mom started paying attention to what I ate or drank, and began to see that I would take drinks of her Fresca. Once that was eliminated, the seizure activity decreased. I still cannot have anything to do with aspartame, or I start to get headaches, and it has led me to other seizures throughout my life.

God had me in His shelter, but Satan had control of my brain, and I started to live with the fear of seizures. I knew that fear was not of the Lord, but it continued to be my companion. What was worse, it became a piece of my identity, and I allowed it to live for many years. It became so much a part of me that I believed it was normal. I think some key scriptures we forget to teach or to talk about are the scriptures on the fear of the Lord. Many of these scriptures are found in the book of Proverbs. Proverbs 3:7 says, "Do not be wise in your own eyes; fear the LORD and shun evil." Proverbs 9:10 says, "The fear of the Lord is the beginning of wisdom, and knowledge of the Holy One is understanding." Proverbs 10:27 states, "The fear of the LORD adds length to life, but the years of the wicked are cut short." Why did I not know I could take my fear and turn it towards the fear of the Lord? To make sure my fear is in the correct category. The Enemy took his fear of the Lord and put it upon me so that I just had fear and was not applying it in the correct area. So now I have learned to alter fear appropriately, and the only thing I fear is not following God correctly or listening to what He tells me to do. So when fear tries to come in to visit, I ask Jesus to answer the door. I run to the shelter of my Father's wing and ask Him what He wants me to do with this. Fear of the Lord brings peace, joy, love, and an overflowing abundance of life. It's a healthy fear, one that guides me appropriately in the direction I am supposed to go.

This led me to start exploring how God's breath was life, but I was focused on death and things that did not bring me freedom. In 2018, I had not had a seizure in four years, but I was going to be taking another licensing test as a counselor, which was the highest license in my state. The stress started to become too much, and it led me to a partial seizure, which then led me to the doctors again. I was a professional who was struggling with old identities. Through my sleep study, the recommendation was that I get counseling, and they did want to potentially start me on medication. I asked them to give me six months and then do another MRI.

It was in that season that I gave God my everything. I laid down the flesh and told Him I was all His. Six months later, when I went and got tested again, the results showed no activity and my brain scan looked so good that it impressed the doctors. That is the power of breathing and praying with God. He literally changed my brain, and the scans were proof. I would love to say that I stayed in breath with Him after that, but unfortunately, new seasons came, and I stopped breathing with Him. We are human and flesh, and we may fall down. What I have learned is how to get back to God way faster and let His amazing grace shine through my story. Getting to the shelter of God's wing has taken time and has come with practice. It has come with utilizing the mindfulness practices within this book and understanding what the Bible truly says.

What I want you to learn from me is that no matter what is occurring in your life, you can either breathe through it with God and get to the other side, or you can choose not to take full breaths and let the Enemy have a say in your story. I think the concept of breathing helps us to remember how much we need God; breathing is constant, and we do it because we are alive. God is constant, and we need Him because we are alive. How are you living? Are you living with God and breathing Him, or are you living without Him and breathing alone?

I want to explore some more areas where the Scripture tells us about breath so that you can truly start to breathe in all the goodness and breathe out all the chaos. Breathing is something we take for granted until we can't. When we have a panic attack, when we hyperventilate, when we are in a seizure, when we sigh in frustration—these are the times we notice our breathing, however, it tends to be in a more negative light. Breath is what connects us; breath is what keeps us together.

There are many verses in Job that reference breath, and I want us to explore them a little more. Job has not always been a book of the Bible that I like to read or look at. I recall seasons in my life questioning if God is giving permission to the Enemy to attack me and telling God I don't want to be like Job. Now I pray that if chaos, trauma, or struggles enter my life, I can be a Job in the midst. I never want to blame God again, and instead ask God what He would like me to change or do with this (whatever the "this" of the moment is).

THE STORY OF JOB AND GOD'S BREATH

Here are some scripture verses from Job that I feel are important for me as I remember God's breath and how to breathe.

- Job 7:18, "He will not let me get my breath, but fills me with bitterness." It is one thing for the Enemy to take my breath, but it is another thing when God takes my breath. Because when God is taking my breath away, it becomes a beautiful area of restoration, healing, and power.

- Job 12:10 (NASB), "In whose hand is the life of every living thing, and the breath of all mankind?" God is the one who allows us to breathe—He determines it all, and He is the breath of us all.

- Job 27:3 (NLT), "For as long as I have life within me, and the breath of God in my nostrils…" For as long as I am living, the breath of God is in my nostrils. Do you know the power behind that? We often wonder where God is, and He is in our next breath. He is in the air we breathe, because that is how He started all mankind.

- Job 32:8 (NKJV), "But it is a spirit in man, and the breath of the Almighty gives them understanding." The Holy Spirit within us gives us breath of the Almighty, and through that we get understanding. Sometimes the understanding is just remembering that God is good and He has good plans for us.

- Job 33:4, "The Spirit of God has made me; the breath of the Almighty gives me life." Look again. We get to see how the Spirit of God made us and gives us life. The very breath you just took is how you know that God is with you in your life.

- Job 34:14–15 (ESV), "If he should set his heart to it and gather to himself his spirit and his breath, all flesh would perish together, and man would return to dust." If God so determined, He could have brought Job back to dust, but instead He took what was lost and made it even better. He took what was broken and restored it. Because Job believed and trusted that He would, and because the Bible clearly tells us God will, we can trust Him.

- Job 37:10–24, "The breath of God produces ice, and the broad waters become frozen. He loads the clouds with moisture; he scatters his lightning through them. At his direction they swirl around over the face of the whole earth to do whatever he commands them. He brings the clouds to punish people, or to water his earth and show his love. 'Listen to this, Job; stop and consider God's wonders. Do you know how God controls the clouds and makes his lightning flash? Do you know how the clouds hang poised, those wonders of him who has perfect knowledge? You who swelter in your clothes when the land lies hushed under the south wind, can you join him in spreading out the skies, hard as a mirror of cast bronze? Tell us what we should say to him; we cannot draw up our case because of our darkness. Should he be told that I want to speak? Would anyone ask to be swallowed up? Now no one can look at the sun, bright as it is in the skies after the wind has swept them clean. Out of the north he comes in golden splendor; God comes in awesome majesty. The Almighty is beyond our reach and exalted in power; in his justice and great righteousness, he does not oppress. Therefore, people revere him, for does he not have regard for all the wise in heart?" Do you see the beauty of all that God can and does do with His breath? How can we not revel in the fact that we are breathing His breath daily?

- Job 41:21 (ESV), "His breath kindles coals, and a flame goes forth from his mouth." He has a power in His breath, and that power we get to breathe, and speak, and defeat the gates of hell.

God's breath is powerful, and it is one of the things we all have in common. If we are alive, we are all breathing. We have power in breath too; the way we breathe can bring calm to our heart, relaxation to our body. The way we speak with our breath can make walls crumble or build walls. There is power in the breath, but our breath will not last forever. His breath will, so let's speak and breathe the word of God upon people so that they may know the power that we have. Job was able to see God even in the storm. Even in his complaints, he saw the goodness of God. He also spoke of the goodness of God, while others attempted to see where Job had gone wrong, he pointed them constantly back to God.

ADDITIONAL SCRIPTURE ON GOD'S BREATH

- Psalms 150:6 (ESV), "Let everything that has breath praise the Lord! Praise the Lord!"

- John 20:22 (ESV), "And when he had said this, he breathed on them and said to them, 'Receive the Holy Spirit.'"

- Isaiah 55:11 (ESV), "So shall my word be that goes out from my mouth; it shall not return to me empty, but it shall accomplish that which I purpose, and shall succeed in the thing for which I sent it."

- 2 Peter 1:21 (ESV), "For no prophecy was ever produced by the will of man, but men spoke from God as they were carried along by the Holy Spirit."

- Isaiah 40:7 (ESV), "The grass withers, the flower fades when the breath of the Lord blows on it; surely the people are grass."

- Isaiah 11:2 (ESV), "And the Spirit of the Lord shall rest upon him, the Spirit of wisdom and understanding, the Spirit of counsel and might, the Spirit of knowledge and the fear of the Lord."

- 2 Samuel 23:2 (ESV), "The Spirit of the Lord speaks by me; his word is on my tongue."

- Psalm 115:17 (ESV), "The dead do not praise the Lord, nor do any who go down in silence."

MINDFULNESS PRACTICE:
BREATHING IN GOD'S LIFE, RELEASING CHAOS

1. Set Your Focus

- Find a quiet space. Sit or stand comfortably. Close your eyes if you feel led.

2. Anchor with Scripture

- Read Job 33:4 (ESV): *"The Spirit of God has made me, and the breath of the Almighty gives me life."*

- Reflect on how God's breath gives you life, purpose, and freedom.

3. Breathe Intentionally

- Inhale slowly and deeply through your nose, imagining God's breath filling you with peace and life.

- Exhale through your mouth, releasing fear, chaos, and everything weighing you down.

- As you breathe, silently say:
  Inhale: "God's breath gives me life."
  Exhale: "I release all chaos to Him."

4. Rest in the Moment

- Spend 1–2 minutes simply breathing, allowing the rhythm of your breath to remind you of God's constant presence.

5. Closing Prayer

- Pray: *"Lord, thank You for Your breath that gives me life. Help me to breathe in Your peace and release all the burdens I carry. Let each breath remind me that You are with me and for me. Amen."*

CHAPTER 5

One-Second Living

"But do not forget this one thing, dear friends: With the Lord a day is like a thousand years, and a thousand years are like a day."

2 Peter 3:8

Do Not Worry About Tomorrow—But What About Today?

Chest tightening, heart palpitations. "Breathe. Breathe. Don't worry about tomorrow, don't worry about tomorrow." Repeating these words to myself, the anxiety grips me deeper, and here I am failing again. *Am I not a Christian? They say you shouldn't be anxious for anything. No one can know. This must be another secret that I must keep, because if this were a normal struggle, Christians would communicate it more.* My head knowledge is a background in psychology, a Master of Science in Counseling. I know this is normal; my heart struggles to accept that this is okay. My heart knows what the sermons have said, my heart knows that I am not in freedom. What do I do? Whom do I tell, how do I reconcile my head and heart? How can this be biblically okay?

I started working on this as if my salvation depended on it. I worked diligently to stay in today. Not worry about tomorrow. Quoting the scriptures daily, learning them, and memorizing them. I was so proud of myself. Until my "today" became unbearable, until the next hour seemed unattainable. Then God. He chose to come and give me a nugget of hope. He chose to whisper gently to me in a way that has brought me freedom. Journey with me as we get into the practice of one-second living.

So Okay...

As I sit down to type these words for this book, I am in a space of *nowhere*, and I am working on my reframe into one second living and allowing myself grace in this space of typing to humbly tell you that I am also here again. Let me explain—as I write this, I cannot hear very well. The night before last, I was woken up by my toddler, only to realize that I felt like my ears were drowning. I felt like I was underwater, but just my ears. I put my son back into bed, and I went to clean my ears, only to notice a unique color on the right side. My eardrums did not burst at this time—I have had my left eardrum burst before, so I know the feeling, but that does not feel like I am underwater. My friend asked me if it felt like I was in a tunnel, and my thoughts were that it felt like I was *nowhere*. I cannot explain how this space feels right now. To hear but feel like I am behind a wall. To not hear to my fullest ability. It is a good reminder to have more gratitude.

As I am navigating this space of being unable to hear, I felt like God said, *Write this too*. Was it to humble myself and remind myself that I can still feel like I am *nowhere*, to help you see that even when you have made progress, you may feel like you are *nowhere*? It is both of those things and many more. I love the knowledge that *nowhere* is a part of me to a level, and I believe it is an area to keep me focused on where I am supposed to be. It now gives me an awareness that I am not being present within myself or with God, and lets me know that I would benefit from doing a self-care practice. I work on doing this practice I created: One-second living daily. It was the only way I could make it through the different things that started occurring.

In 2019, I was navigating many spaces within myself and my *nowhere*. I was living in the scripture verse that says not to worry about tomorrow, for tomorrow has enough worries of its own (Matthew 6:34). I was doing so well at not worrying about tomorrow, but everything within the day was a worry. Tomorrow's worries, though, I allowed to stay in tomorrow. Finally, I was only worrying about the day! It took me such a long time to get down to just a day's worth of worries, so give yourself grace as you learn to live one second at a time.

So, then I came across the Bible verse that tells us that a day to us could be like a year to God. 2 Peter 3:8 (NLT) says, "But you must not forget this one thing, dear friends: A day is like a thousand years to the Lord, and a thousand years is like a day." The Lord is not really being slow about his promise, as some people think. No, he is being patient for your sake. He does not want anyone to be destroyed, but wants everyone to repent. I felt like God whispered to my heart and said to me, "Your tomorrows are your next seconds, so let's start living one second at a time."

It became my new practice, and by practice, I mean I started doing it daily, and I still do it. Sometimes it is just a deep breath in and out and saying "one second" or "Jesus," recalibrating my brain and staying in the present moment. It has helped my brain slow down, breathe, and think. Not only are His mercies new every day, but His mercies are new every second. His grace covers all, and I can learn to live in the moment with Him as my guide.

One-second living has made my days easier, and my thought processes have been rewired and renewed. Neuroscientist Dr. Jill Bolte Taylor has shown that emotions tend to come and go in only 90 seconds if we can identify the internal experience, name the emotions, and allow them to flow out of us.[6] So, an emotion comes, and I can breathe, embrace, love, and allow God to rewrite the emotion into something that brings Him glory and honor. As I breathe, I like to look up, so that I am doing an action for the scripture that tells us to set your mind on things above (Colossians 3:2).

I feel like one-second living also comes with the ability to hear. To hear the still small voice, to cultivate enough stillness that God's voice can flow over you. I feel like my literal inability to hear at this time is a perfect example of when I was blocked from God, not because of God, but because of what I was allowing the Enemy to do within my thoughts. When I had separated myself from God to protect myself, I only ended up being unprotected. I want you right now to start slowing down to hear God's voice, to know that He is present and near and that He is in your every *nowhere*, somewhere, or anywhere. He has always been. If you cannot hear His voice yet, then I would challenge you to go read the Bible, and maybe start in Psalms. He speaks to us in such beautiful and loving ways through His Word.

Right now, I want you to take a deep breath in through your nose and out through your mouth. Allow your lungs to fill fully and then release, and I want you to think or say, "One second." We do not have to wait until tomorrow for a fresh start, for a new emotion or feeling. We can embrace this moment, breathe in Jesus, release anything weighing us down, and go to "one-second living" with Him.

---

6 Taylor, Jill Bolte. "My Stroke of Insight." 2008, https://www.ted.com/speakers/jill_bolte_taylor.

I just got a moment to practice some one-second living. My toddler, who should already be asleep, which is why I am doing my writing, showed up at my bedroom door. I pick him up and he asks me if I can rock him. I rock him and hold him and co-regulate with him. I breathe deep and allow this to be a give-and-take in our mother-son relationship, versus me just giving. Breathing it in and smiling at these seconds with my son is a continuation of my growth. It is very easy to focus on the next thing to do, and I was busy writing, but in that moment, I had a God interruption and spent it wisely with the one-second moment of allowing my child to be comforted by me while I took comfort in him.

Do you need to take comfort in God? He calls you to rest in Him, He calls you to lie in green pastures, He calls you to still waters. He will restore your soul (Psalm 23:1–3).

2 Peter 3 is a good chapter in its wholeness. Although God whispered to me some things to help me in daily life, it also helps me slow down other aspects of life. I want to be like Jesus, and therefore, I want to understand that God wants to make sure everyone has an opportunity to come to Jesus, so He is taking time to bring us home to Him. He wants everyone to be in Heaven with Him, and I want that, too.

Because I want to be more like Jesus, and I want to make sure I am being present wherever I am, I have chosen to become more outspoken in my personal life in areas that, in the past, I would have put headphones in and ignored. I now walk into Walmart, and I look for opportunities to make others smile, to send a prayer to someone, and to be a kind person. I want to be able to live so much like Jesus that people only think of Him when they think of me.

When I heard the song "One Awkward Moment" by Casting

Crowns, it really changed how I approach different situations and became an added part to my one-second living. The lyrics challenge us to step out of our comfort zone and into people's stories.[7]

I am not sure the masks I wore would have shown anyone that I needed the awkward moment. I needed someone to come in and tell me that God still loved me. I needed someone to combat what I grew up hearing, so that I knew that someone else's sin upon me didn't mean I was tainted. I also needed to know that the sins I chose to then fall into, God could redeem those, too. The masks I wore were beautifully cultivated from a broken vessel into a culturally appropriate face. So, the awkward moments could be for the girl you can tell is broken, or the one who is masking well. It's not your job to know when to have an awkward moment; you just get to listen to His voice. Please have the awkward moments, you could save a life.

---

7 Casting Crowns. "One Awkward Moment." *Casting Crowns*, written by Mark Hall and Seth Mosley, Sony Music Entertainment, 2018. YouTube, https://www.youtube.com/watch?v=n_IBVPFvNVQ.

MINDFULNESS PRACTICE: ONE-SECOND LIVING

Exercise 1: Embracing the Present

1. Read and Reflect:

- Open your Bible to Matthew 6:34: *"Therefore do not worry about tomorrow, for tomorrow will worry about itself. Each day has enough trouble of its own."*

- Then read 2 Peter 3:8: *"With the Lord a day is like a thousand years, and a thousand years are like a day."*

2. Pause and Realize:

- Our next second could be our tomorrow. Say aloud: *"One second."*

3. Stay Present:

- Lovingly focus your mind on the "One second."

- Pray: *"Lord, remove the burdens of the next seconds and keep me grounded in this moment."*

Exercise 2: Breathing in Love

1. Focus on Your Breath:

- Breathe deeply in through your nose and out through your mouth.

2. Connect with Your Heart:

- Place your hand on your heart as you continue to breathe deeply.

3. Speak or Sing Truths:

- Sing or say: *"Jesus loves me, this I know, for the Bible tells me so."*

- Say: *"I am worthy because of Jesus."*

4. Anchor the Reminder:

- Repeat to yourself: *"One second at a time."*

- Write it down in a visible place to remember throughout your day.

Exercise 3: Releasing Anxiety Through Gratitude

1. Read and Reflect:

- Reflect on Philippians 4:6: *"Do not be anxious about anything, but in every situation, by prayer and petition, with thanksgiving, present your requests to God."*

2. Accept and Release Anxiety:

- Acknowledge that anxiety is not inherently bad as long as it is brought to God in prayer.

3. Focus on Gratitude:

- Search for the goodness in your life. Gratitude has the power to ease worries.

- Write down one or more things you are thankful for. Consider starting a Gratitude Jar or Journal to build this habit.

4. Extend Grace to Yourself:

- Remind yourself that these practices take time and repetition to become healthy habits. Give yourself grace as you grow.

CHAPTER 6

Surrender = Actually Okay = Godly Direction

How Can I Surrender?

How can I be me when the *me* that I am is either not liked or the cause of the chaos? How do I surrender when all I want is control? If I surrender, does that mean worse can occur to me? Because I've humbled myself, I've softened my heart and let myself be available to more pain. If I don't surrender, can I still follow God? Surrender is what my body did when the seizures occurred. Surrender is what my head did when the voices could be heard. Surrender is what my body did when the assault occurred. To choose surrender sounds harmful. Sounds scary, sounds unsafe. Trying to protect myself has not been working. What if I do surrender to a safe place? I am now aware of those surrenders the Enemy stole by making surrendering to God seem scary. In not surrendering to God to protect me, I became unprotected, and it got a lot more exhausting to become "good enough" to earn salvation.

OKAY THEN

In a world where authenticity has become cliché, how do we honestly become okay and have it mean something to people? We go anywhere, and people ask us questions like, "How are you?" "Are you okay?" "How is your day?" Our answers are very vague, even in the church. Why? What does "okay" mean, and why are people utilizing it all the time, especially if it is not the truth?

Merriam-Webster Dictionary defines okay as "fine, in a satisfactory way; as in, you did OK on that last test."[8]

Does the Bible say that we are only going to live an okay life or that we were only meant to be okay? John 10:10 tells us that we get to have an abundant life here on earth. Is that what we mean when we say we are okay or fine? I can only answer for myself. When I say I am okay, that means I am not fully great, but not fully bad. When I say "I am fine," I am referring to the acronym of F.I.N.E., a line in the movie *The Italian Job*, which stands for Freaked out, Insecure, Neurotic, and Emotional.[9] I have told people that if that is my answer, then I am very far away from okay.

As a follower of Christ, how would I like to start answering those questions and be more authentic? I was given words of wisdom many years ago from my brother; he stated to answer appropriately and truthfully, and then give praise to God. I have learned to be true in my answer and no longer be generic. So if I am asked, I will maybe say, "Today was a little tiring, but God is good and I am so grateful for His strength and energy." I am always trying to praise. I have had to learn to actually be okay with not being okay.

Plumb's song "Exhale" has the lyrics, "It's okay to not be okay,

---

8   "America's Most Trusted Dictionary." *Merriam-Webster*, www.merriam-webster.com. Accessed Oct. 2024.

9   Gray, F. Gary, director. *The Italian Job*. Paramount Pictures, 2003.

this is a safe place."[10] To learn that it was okay to not be okay, but to then think, "*hmmm, I am actually okay?*" The song talks about surrender, and surrender brings us to a place where we are actually okay, even in a story where maybe we shouldn't be okay. Surrender brings us to a place where we are finally able to stand in the "I" (eye) of the storm and remember the I Am. In the "I" we can see the world spinning and the story unfolding, but we are safe and actually okay, even when the world thinks we couldn't be.

Surrender leads us to being actually okay, authentically okay, which then leads us into God's direction.

Before I researched the acronym F.I.N.E. from *The Italian Job* to make sure I had it correct for this book, I had always thought the letter "N" stood for "narcissistic" instead of "neurotic." Deciding to use this acronym has caused this chapter to take turns I did not expect from referencing the word "narcissistic". I was not going to discuss such a taboo word, especially when I think about my career. The amount of people who come in and tell me about the other people in their lives who are "narcissistic" I do not have enough hands to count. When the person is a Christian, I can utilize the scripture verse about not looking at the splinter within someone else's eye but seeing the log within our own. I identify that we are all human and God has warned us against our selfishness—if all we do is focus on how the other person needs to change and they are not the one in therapy, then the client will have no way to profoundly move forward. I, in and of myself, believe that narcissism is just an innovative word for an old sin that comes from the deceiver of deception and lies to make us believe that we are allowed to be selfish. I remember when people used to identify with

---

10   Plumb. *Exhale*. Word Records and Curb Records, 2015. YouTube, https://www.youtube.com/watch?v=dOgUjSW4agg.

what they did in their relationships and what they contributed. Now what I hear is what others do *not* do and what others are *not* contributing. Our selfishness is real, and our sinful nature is real. I know from my own selfishness. Because of the first sin, we are all a little broken, a little wounded, and a little lost in *nowhere*. We then self-protect; we may become selfish. It makes sense, and it is understandable, especially when people have experienced trauma. The truth I learned is that it was one thing to feel like I needed to protect myself from others, but it was another matter when I was protecting myself from God the Father, Jesus, and the Holy Spirit. This was not a conscious thought—I did not just one day say, "I protect myself from the Trinity"—it was a slow decline, and it took a lot of self-growth for me to fully be all parts of me with the Trinity. They have loved me through it all. They never forced me back, but They called to me and when I went to Them, there was no shame or condemnation but complete mercy and grace as They lavished a love on me I had never fully known and maybe cannot even explain completely. That's a love that I hope is experienced for all the people who feel like they are *nowhere,* as they get to the place of *now here.* I pray your *now here* is not just accepting your literal position but embracing a spiritual stance of the *now here* in the Father's arms of unconditional love and positive regard. Dr. David Nichols of Our Father's Heart ministry stated, "God does not just love you; He likes you!"[11]

I want all of us to be authentic, but not in the excusing behavior that allows us to get away with not changing our ways to become more like Jesus. I want to make sure I am a sheep in this world and that I know my Father's voice. There were times when I struggled with pieces of who I was, but I was authentic about

---

11 Nichols, David. Heart of the Father Ministries, Williston, ND, 25 June 2024.

them, and that was just who I am, or what I was, or a genetic trait. I want you to be able to grasp godly authenticity to make sure that you are leading people to Christ and not away from Him. When we don't share the darkness or the storms with one another, especially after healing and freedom, we are not opening ourselves up to being vessels that Jesus can use to help others in their darkness and storms—those who guide with love and truth, even when it is hard to do so. Speaking in truth is one of the greatest ways to love one another. To speak the truth, we need to know the truth, so we should study the Bible to speak those truths aloud. My prayer is that God will always help me to be able to speak truth, even when fear may come, so that I can be more like Jesus and guide people closer to Him.

I want our answers to become honest, for us to not say, "I am okay" if we are struggling, but to always make sure we bring God praise. Now that we have a little more understanding of this, let's go into our next mindfulness practice to teach us how to surrender to God's direction. If we are honest and start in the valley, then when we give God glory, we go to the mountaintop.

MINDFULNESS PRACTICE:
SURRENDERING TO GOD'S DIRECTION

1. Set the Scene

- Find a quiet place where you can reflect without distractions. Close your eyes and take a deep breath.

2. Anchor in Scripture

- Read John 10:10 aloud: *"The thief comes only to steal and kill and destroy; I have come that they may have life, and have it to the full."*

- Reflect on how God promises an abundant life, even when you feel "okay" or less than fine.

3. Acknowledge Your Current State

- Ask yourself: *"How am I really?"*

- Write down or speak aloud an honest response, even if it's messy or difficult to admit.

4. Surrender Through Prayer

- Pray: *"Lord, I surrender my 'okay' to You. Help me step into Your strength and truth. I praise You for Your love, even when I feel weak or unsure. Guide me toward Your abundant life."*

5. Reframe with Praise

- Practice reframing your emotions by saying something like:
  "Today is hard, but God is good, and I'm leaning on His strength."
  "I'm overwhelmed, but I trust in the peace that only God can give."

6. Close in Stillness

- Take a few deep breaths, imagining yourself in the "I" of the storm, where the "I Am" holds you securely.

CHAPTER 7

You're Here

Remember how I said I longed for a sign saying "You are here" in my life, much like one you'd find on a hiking trail? But what does the "You are here" mean if I am unsure where I want to go? Maps—whether for a hiking trail, a state, a mall, or a journey through life—always offer multiple paths and spaces. The direction we choose depends on where we want to end up.

In the same way, I've often wished for a spiritual map with a "You are here" marker to guide me. It would make it so much easier to know where I am and what direction to take. So, how do we get to where we want to be if we don't know where we are and where we're going? "You are here" gives you an idea of which direction to take, but only if you know your goal.

I had to figure out my goals and recognize the areas in my life where I felt like I was *nowhere*. Those spaces became the stepping stones that brought me to my "*now here*" moments. So, what is your goal? What is your path? You are here reading this chapter, and maybe you are hoping I'll tell you where to go or what to do.

But I can't do that because I don't know your goals or your story. What I can do is share what I've learned about seeking clarity and purpose in my own life.

For much of my life, I had goals—some as a child, some as an adult—but they didn't account for the finite details of life. This left me scrambling and fearful of making the wrong choices. I had to stop focusing so much on daily details and the big choices and instead look at the bigger picture of what I was moving toward. My prayer became, "God, please help me where I am, so that I can get to where You are." This prayer marked a turning point in understanding how my current "You are here" moment could align with God's greater purpose. A knowledge that God is always here, wherever the "here" is.

It took me years to realize that my career, while fulfilling, wasn't my ultimate purpose. My purpose, my goal, my destination—the point I want to reach on the map—is my heavenly home. This realization helped me recalibrate so many areas of my life. Once I saw that as my true goal, so many other decisions fell into place because I now had a standard to guide me. Thank God that all I must do is obey and follow Him. Thank God that with Him I am never lost but always found. That even in my flesh, He still loves me and continues to perfect me.

This recalibration required me to stop focusing on achievements or circumstances and start focusing on who I am in God. He showed me that I am His—that He holds me in the palm of His hand, smiles upon me, and calls me His daughter. He reminded me that my purpose is to praise and worship Him, to celebrate Him daily, and to give Him all the glory.

THE OLD TESTAMENT AND GOD'S DETAILED PLANS

Just as maps guide us, the Old Testament provides intricate

details that reflect God's plans and directions for our lives. Let's take a closer look. In Jeremiah 29:11, God says, "'For I know the plans I have for you,' declares the Lord, 'plans to prosper you and not to harm you, plans to give you hope and a future.'" This verse assures us that God has good plans for each of us. Though He doesn't write out our individual stories in the Bible, the details He gives us about the Tabernacle and the Ark of the Covenant show us the care He puts into His plans.

During a recent Bible study on the Old Testament, my small group discussed why God included so many details about the Tabernacle. If God included so many details about the Tabernacle and His purpose for it, how much more does He have in store for us, His physical temple bearers? It may take time to understand His plans, and they might not always make sense to us. But just as the Tabernacle and the Ark of the Covenant were carefully designed, our lives are also a part of His beautiful and intentional story.

NOW THAT WE ARE HERE – HOW DO WE BRING HEAVEN DOWN?

As I stated, my purpose, goal, destination, and the area I want to get to on the map is my heavenly home. That is beautiful, right? But maybe a little too cliché for you. Or maybe it makes you sad because you are not in Heaven yet. Trust me, I feel you and I get you. I look forward to the day I get to be in the Father's full presence. But we get to have Heaven now, I have that now, and I want you to have that now. I want you to know the freedom I have searched for and continue to stay in daily. For the past few years, God has continued to bring the scripture to mind about abundant life. Sounds pretty. Sounds good, but also sounded unattainable for me.

To be honest, it *is* unattainable to me in my own strength, but

God. Because of what God did for us by sending His Son, we can have abundant life, every single one of us. It is not just a promise for me, but a promise for us all. So, how do we get there? For me, it was first acknowledging that I have not been living an abundant life mindset. Second was believing that I could have one here and now no matter the circumstances. Trusting Jesus that everything He did was enough so that I could also live in freedom. I love getting there daily and becoming more like Jesus because His mercies are new every day. What I love even more is helping others step into that place, too. To watch as clients let God break off chains of the past, of genetics, of their own sin, or generational sin. To see the looks on their faces when they are finally closer to where they want to be, and understand it was not because of what they have or have not done, but because of who Jesus is. It is a beautiful space. I pray that along with the Word of God, my testimony can help you on your journey of getting *now here*.

PEOPLE OF THE BIBLE

JOSEPH'S JOURNEY: FROM *NOWHERE* TO *NOW HERE*

The Bible is filled with stories of individuals who journeyed through "*nowhere*" moments before stepping into their "*now here*." One of the most compelling examples is Joseph. As a young man, Joseph was favored by his father, which sparked jealousy among his brothers. He was mocked, thrown into a pit, sold into slavery, and falsely accused—all "*nowhere*" moments that could have broken him. Yet, through it all, Joseph stayed faithful to God.

Despite his circumstances, Joseph chose to be present and serve where he was. He didn't let the "*nowhere*" moments define him. Instead, he allowed God to work through them, ultimately becoming Pharaoh's right-hand man and saving countless lives during a famine. Joseph's story reminds us that even when we feel stuck or lost, God is working to bring us into a place of purpose and abundance. This was also a part of the grand narrative of the Bible for God's chosen people to be rescued and not die from famine.

Something recently stood out to me about Joseph that I believe God wants you to hear. It is what his brothers said about him: "Oh look, here comes the dreamer!" (Genesis 37:19; adapted). As I spent personal time with God and in His Word, I felt like God whispered to my heart and said, "All of My children have been dreamers." He gave me insight to see that adult Christians, when they were children, had dreams and believed before the Enemy stole their dreams and beliefs because he is a thief that wants to destroy the good things God gives you (John 10:10). After that time of prayer and fellowship with God, I feel like He wants you to know a couple of things if that is your story.

First, you are not a mistake; you are chosen. Second, you were made in the image of God. That is your identity. Third, children are so important to God that He states it clearly in the scriptures. Mark 10:13–16 says, "People were bringing little children to Jesus for him to place his hands on them, but the disciples rebuked them. When Jesus saw this, he was indignant. He said to them, 'Let the little children come to me, and do not hinder them, for the kingdom of God belongs to such as these.'" In Matthew 18:2–6,

He called a little child to him, and placed the child among them. And he said: 'Truly I tell you, unless you change and become like little children, you will never enter the kingdom of heaven. Therefore, whoever takes the lowly position of this child is the greatest in the kingdom of heaven. And whoever welcomes one such child in my name welcomes me. If anyone causes one of these little ones—those who believe in me—to stumble, it would be better for them to have a large millstone hung around their neck and to be drowned in the depths of the sea.

The fourth thing to know is that God welcomes us to come to Him like children, as His sons and daughters. **Joseph was somewhere of importance. Then he was *nowhere*. He chose even in the *nowhere* to be *now here*.**

DAVID'S JOURNEY: FROM *NOWHERE* TO *NOW HERE*

Like Joseph, David's journey also took him through "*nowhere*" moments that refined his character and strengthened his faith. David was a shepherd boy. He was strong in that he fought bears and lions, but was not looked upon by his family. Before one of his first famous stories, Samuel is told that he will find the next king through the family of Jesse, who was David's father. Jesse had all his sons come except David, but God did not want them. Saul asks if there is another son, and Jesse then has David come. God looked at David's heart. Others may have overlooked David, or may have overlooked you, but God never does. He sees past what others do, and He sees your heart.

Later, David's father sent him to feed his brothers, and he witnessed no one brave enough to fight the giant Goliath, who was mocking them. He said he would fight him. The king attempted to put him in armor that was the wrong size, but David had the spiritual armor of the Lord. He grabbed his sling and five rocks. He only needed the one. He won the war by believing in God more than himself or anything else. He then went back to being a shepherd. He returned to ordinary life for a while, until God strategically positioned him in the kingdom as a servant. He was in the castle, which was meant to be his, but he was just waiting for his time. David became a musician for Saul, and he was best friends with Saul's son Jonathan. Saul had a spirit of anger towards him and started to try to kill him. David had to run; he ran away from Saul for many years. David had the opportunity to take matters into his own hands a few different times, and instead, he waited upon the Lord to fulfill what the Lord had promised. Finally, Saul passed away, and the kingdom became David's. On his way to rule, God stopped him in Hebron, and he ruled there for 7 years. From the time when Samuel anointed him to be the future king to when he became king was probably over fifteen years. In all the *nowhere*s of his story, David stayed faithful, and we know that he was considered a man after God's own heart (1 Samuel 16:1–13; 1 Samuel 17; 1 Samuel 18–31; 2 Samuel 1–5; Psalm 23; Psalm 51; Acts 13:22). The Psalms, which David contributed to writing, are one of my favorite books of the Bible for navigating the emotional spaces of *nowhere*.

David was a shepherd boy who let the Lord use him and mature him into the man he became. He was a man after God's own heart.

URIAH'S JOURNEY: FROM *NOWHERE* TO *NOW HERE*

While David's journey showcases perseverance, Uriah's story reminds us of the importance of staying faithful even when others fail us. Uriah's story is a little different, but it is intertwined with King David's. Uriah was a mighty warrior. He was one of the King's men. Uriah was out fighting in the war when King David asked about his wife, Bathsheba. King David had an affair with her, and she became pregnant. He then sent for Uriah to come to visit under the ruse that he wanted to know how they were faring in the war. Uriah came and spent time with the King. The King then sent him home in the hopes that he would have relations with his wife, so that King David would be free from being found out. Uriah was such a man of God that he wouldn't have a good evening knowing that his men were out there fighting. So, he slept at the castle door. King David then sent him back with a note sealed for someone else that says to send Uriah to the front lines and then pull back, which is how Uriah was killed. King David's son with Bathsheba was taken from this earth due to King David's sin. Uriah, in his *nowhere* stayed faithful to his call. To his mission. Although his story has an untimely end due to the sin of another, I believe that his choices cultivated a beautiful reward for him in Heaven. He did not succumb to temptation or pleasure when he knew what his mission was. He stayed focused and persevered, and God had his back even after death. King David sinned, but he turned back to God with a repentant heart. That's why Scripture tells us he was a "man after his own heart"—not because he was perfect, but because God knew David's heart would return to Him, even after failure (2 Samuel 11; 2 Samuel 12:1–25; 1 Samuel 13:14; Acts 13:22). I added Uriah's story because sometimes in our *nowheres,* all we can see is the other person's sin upon our lives. Uriah did not know what was going on. Too often, the Enemy lets us know what is happening in our lives, and we lose focus on what God is calling us into.

Uriah was a warrior, a mighty man. He did not allow temptation to lead him astray, and he stayed focused on the mission at hand.

Each of these men—Joseph, David, and Uriah—faced moments of uncertainty and hardship, yet their faithfulness in the "*nowhere*" allowed God to lead them to their "*now here*." Their stories remind us that we can trust God's plans even when we don't see the full picture.

MINDFULNESS PRACTICE: YOU ARE HERE

1. Set the Scene

- Find a quiet space where you won't be interrupted. Sit comfortably with a piece of paper or your phone's notepad.

2. Acknowledge Your Location

- Write down where you are in each of these areas:

    Literal Space: Where are you physically?

    Emotional Space: What emotions are you feeling right now?

    Physical Space: How does your body feel?

    Spiritual Space: Where do you feel you are in your walk with God?

3. Identify Contentment

- Reflect on each area. Ask yourself: *Am I at peace with this space? Why or why not?*

4. Invite God into the Space

- Close your eyes and imagine God meeting you exactly where you are. Pray: *"Lord, thank You for being here with me. Help me to see Your purpose in this moment and trust Your guidance for where I'm going."*

5. Declare Your Presence

- Speak aloud or write: *"You are here."* Let this reminder ground you in the present moment.

6. Breathe and Release

- Take a deep breath in, imagining God's peace filling you. Exhale, releasing any worry or fear about what's next.

CHAPTER 8

Focus Where?

BACK THEN

Focus. Focus. The voices are yelling within my head again, drowning out any voice of truth. I'm supposed to be playing kick the can, and I'm in charge of protecting the can. If I focus on the voices, they say words that bring no peace. If I focus on the game, then I can do this. I was a child who did not understand what was occurring in my head. Focusing on external things allowed me a break from the internal warfare that was occurring. I referenced the voices earlier, but they continued to haunt me throughout my life. The voices started around the age of three; they weren't always mean, but they were constant. The night terrors happened around four, so now daytime was difficult, and when sleep came, it was worse. My God-fearing parents took me seriously when I stated, "They are biting me." They were able to pray, and God led them to what needed to be removed from our house. I feel like those stories would need their own book or blog post.

Once those stopped, seizures began. I no longer felt like focusing could be on anything in this world. Poetry, journaling, and reading became my escape. If I were reading, I was focused. When I was given the scripture of where we should focus, "On whatever is true, lovely, pure, admirable," I felt like my head was unable to find truth or stay grounded (Philippians 4:8). Focusing above did not work when the enemy of my soul had made the spiritual realms fearful.

HERE WE ARE

As I sit here to write this, I find it interesting that my focus is not where I want it. That I am merely writing because I gave myself a goal of writing weekly, and that I have people who will check in on that goal. If we put our focus *nowhere*, we will certainly be focused on things that do not matter.

The Bible says in Colossians 3:2 (ESV), "Set your mind on things above, not on things that are on earth." However, I think the key question for this chapter and those reading it, even me at this moment, is: How?

How do we set our thoughts on things above when things right now feel out of control or uncontrollable? These two words mean the same thing and yet are so completely different. Webster's Dictionary defines "control" as

> a : to exercise restraining or directing influence over : REGULATE
>
> *control one's anger*
>
> b: to have power over : RULE

The definition of "uncontrollable" is

> 1. incapable of being controlled : UNGOVERNABLE.
>   *a rush of uncontrollable emotions*

2. archaic: free from control by a superior power : AB-SOLUTE[12]

Do you see this? Do you see some of the keywords that Merriam-Webster wrote in all capital letters? They chose to put those words in capitals, I am just choosing to quote them like they did. Let's look at those words a little more.

Regulate. Rule. Ungovernable. Absolute.

We look around for focus—what can I control—regulate, or rule. So, then we start to feel like we or everything else is uncontrollable, ungovernable, or absolute. What happens when we try to regulate or govern our own lives? We have become dysregulated and ungovernable.

As a counselor, I sometimes work with clients who are grasping and holding onto things that they feel are in their control, which can very easily lead them into becoming out of control and ungovernable. With the brain having now been wired this way, they then struggle and will not let me guide them, but more importantly, they will not let God guide them. When we have no clue what we are holding onto, we can start to frantically search for anything or anyone to rescue us. It may be that we are already out of control and are struggling to regulate ourselves.

God gave us some key scriptures to help, but do not just say them once; do not say them in your thoughts. Memorize them and speak them aloud with your God-given authority as a son or daughter of the one true King. Philippians 4:8 (ESV) says, "Finally, brothers, whatever is true, whatever is honorable, whatever is just, whatever is pure, whatever is lovely, whatever is commendable, if there is any excellence, if there is anything worthy of praise, think

---

12 *America's Most Trusted Dictionary.*" Merriam-Webster, Merriam-Webster, www.merriam-webster.com/. Accessed December 2024.

about these things."

In the midst of my *nowhere,* I could not see these things. This verse was pretty and held powerful insights, but even with those insights, I was blinded by my traumas. The questions would flow through my thoughts—*How, God? How do I see these things when I am wounded and hurting? How, God, do I see this? How?* I was looking at myself through the lens of this verse and not looking at God.

When I was able to separate myself from the pain of yesterday into the promise of today and look for God's truth, honor, purity, loveliness, commendability, excellence, and praiseworthiness, I moved forward. I was able to focus on that verse, but I had to lovingly release myself, not lose myself, but release myself into the embrace of God the Father, Jesus the Son, and the Holy Spirit.

Then the things of the past became clear—God is not the author of the trauma or the sin upon my life, but He is the one who has redeemed me, saved me, raised me up, kept me strong, and protected me even if circumstances did not change. He took off the glasses I was wearing that showed me the world from a human perspective and gave me heavenly glasses through which I can now see more clearly and discern a little bit better to see how God wants me in His story for my life. He brought me to the end of myself, and in that space, He brought restoration and taught me how to refocus and see through His glasses.

Colossians 3:1–4 (ESV) says, "If then you have been raised with Christ, seek the things that are above, where Christ is, seated at the right hand of God. Set your minds on things that are above, not on the things that are on earth. For you have died, and your life is hidden in Christ in God. When Christ who is your life appears, then you also will appear with him in glory."

See how much richer this passage is when you grab a few more verses? We are raised with Christ, we are hidden with Christ in God. I thought I died when my trauma occurred, but the reality was I planted, and as I let God water the soil and remove the garden of death, I died to myself and rose in Christ.

Let us explore some other ideas of changing our focus from Romans 8:6–8 (ESV), "For to set the mind on the flesh is death, but to set the mind on the Spirit is life and peace. For the mind that is set on the flesh is hostile to God, for it does not submit to God's law; indeed, it cannot. Those who are in the flesh cannot please God."

Oof–I, in my flesh, turned hostile towards God after my trauma of sexual assault. Do not get me wrong, I was still seeking my faith and attending church. I had a relationship with Jesus, but I shut God and the Holy Spirit out. I spiraled for many years and harmed myself with premarital relationships. I could not understand why God, who is all-powerful, would allow this to happen to me—but then again, He also allowed Jesus to die. So, I felt like I could connect with Jesus but not with God.

I was hurt. I was a good Christian girl. I was in my senior year of college and deciding what master's program I would go into to do what God had called me to do. The guy was a friend—I was naive to think friends were safe. I was 22 years old, following the path God had for me when this occurred. I did not know what to do with the fact that the friend quoted scripture to me afterwards and then told me God would forgive me. So, I became silent. But worse than my silence was how I became distant from God. I see how Satan played a role now, I see how the verbiage of the guy also created separation in that relationship. I also know why people start to not trust God. My land of *nowhere* became worse, and I spiraled. The only focus I had was: *Do what God wants you to do and become a counselor.* When I see how I still chose to follow God,

I am amazed at where I am now, and how He truly can take all things and make them good.

So, I focused on school, focused on my master's, but I did not focus on the things above. I was in the worst space of *nowhere* I had ever been. Depression and anxiety started to become my identity, and there I was, *nowhere* and "abandoned" by God. He never left me or forsook me, but in my story, I abandoned Him. I walked away from the only area of solace that could have healed me. I walked alone, and I masked in a way that was a beautiful lie to not only the world, but unfortunately, even more so to myself.

It was many years before I truly started to understand that my focus was wrong. God is not the author of sin; Satan is, and I had been letting Satan continue to author my story. He authored the sin, a human did the sin, but I let him continue to be the author of my life. I thought I had taken the pen and was authoring my story now and letting Jesus in, but the reality was in my flesh, Satan was authoring an even bigger spiral so that I could never focus because I just kept falling in circles.

Nowhere.

The circles and the spiral felt like something I've experienced in the literal sense, but in a worse emotional way. Have you ever gone down a spiral slide? It is hard to see, right? So, how do we focus when we are spinning? Some of it may be that counseling is the right avenue for you, finding someone to help you learn how to stop the spiral slide. For others, it may be asking for prayer from safe people. It might be joining a group. Getting involved at church. For me, it was a little bit of everything. I did not at that time have the brain that could just focus and be still, but God did. Through prayer, support, counseling, love, friends, God, Jesus, and the Holy Spirit, I now know how to be still and focus, but it took a lot of different things to rewire what the Enemy had wired. I believe a lot of the reason we are all able to rewire is not because of what we do or don't do, but when we remember who wired us in the beginning and who knew us before we were ever born.

My past is not erased; it is a part of me. I am thankful for my story and can see how God can take anything and make it beautiful. How the story is God's story and not my story. How His ways are higher than my ways. The empathy that I have always had has grown stronger because of my story. God's love for people flows into me no matter who they are. I see people through God's eyes, and for all of that, I am grateful. I also know that something that could have forever torn me from God is what knitted me closer to Him than I could have ever imagined.

As you have been reading, my prayer for you is that you allow yourself to get to the end of yourself and to get off the spiral and let Jesus meet you. A friend stated to me, "You can either hurt with Jesus and get towards healing, or you hurt alone and let Satan win." To die to my flesh is helpful for my focus, because then I can see what God wants me to see and focus on things above. It is a lot prettier when I look at things like God does. I want to reiterate something, too—God did not author sin in my life, but God took the sin that was done and has made my life beautiful, and He can do the same for you!

So Now We Can Focus

A scripture passage that reminds me to not stay focused on the world is the story of when the king of Aram tried to capture Elisha from prophesying and thwarting his battle attempts against Israel.

'Go, find out where he is,' the king ordered, 'so I can send men and capture him.' The report came back: 'He is in Dothan.' Then he sent horses and chariots and a strong force there. They went by night and surrounded the city. When the servant of the man of God got up and went out early the next morning, an army with horses and chariots had surrounded the city. 'Oh no, my lord! What shall we do?' the servant asked. 'Don't be afraid,' the prophet answered. 'Those who are with us are more than those who are with them.' And Elisha prayed, 'Open his eyes, Lord, so that he may see.' Then the Lord opened the servant's eyes, and he looked and saw the hills full of horses and chariots of fire all around Elisha. As the enemy came down toward him, Elisha prayed to the Lord, 'Strike this army with blindness.' So he struck them with blindness, as Elisha had asked. Elisha told them, 'This is not the road, and this is not the city. Follow me, and I will lead you to the man you are looking for.' And he led them to Samaria. (2 Kings 6:13–19)

When you stay focused on what the world shows you, you will stay lost. When you ask God to open your eyes and guide you to where He wants you to be, you will be found and be reminded that Jesus has already won, and we get to sit in victory with Him. We are surrounded by God's protective angels, and like we discussed in Chapter 3, we just need to give them permission to fight.

As we step into this moment of mindfulness, let's embrace the beauty of being fully present in God's truth that we must lean not on our own understanding and focus instead on where He tells us to be.

MINDFULNESS PRACTICE: FOCUS HERE

Let's embrace the beauty of being fully present in this moment as we step into this mindfulness practice.

1. Set your heart in a position to receive. If possible, find a peaceful place in nature to deepen your connection.

2. Read this scripture (Philippians 4:8) out loud:
   "Finally, brothers and sisters, whatever is true, whatever is noble, whatever is right, whatever is pure, whatever is lovely, whatever is admirable—if anything is excellent or praise-worthy—think about such things."

3. Identify areas of focus.

Focus on What is True

- You were made in God's image.

- You're loved just because of who you are.

- You're worthy because Jesus died for you.

- You're an heir of God's kingdom.

- You're a child of God.

- Your sins have been paid for.

(Pause and reflect: Which of these truths speaks most deeply to your heart today?)

Focus on What is Noble

- Jesus died for you.

- He lived a perfect life.

- He died knowing you would struggle.

- He freed you because of His great love.

(Pause and reflect: How can you live nobly in response to His love?)

Focus on What is Right

- You are clothed in Jesus' righteousness.
- There is no condemnation for those in Christ.

(Pause and reflect: How can you walk confidently in this righteousness today?)

Focus on What is Pure

- God's love is pure and unfailing.
- Your thoughts can reflect His purity when guided by the Spirit.
- Pure intentions flow from a heart surrendered to His will.

(Pause and reflect: What steps can you take to purify your thoughts and actions?)

Focus on What is Lovely

- The beauty of God's creation—the trees, the sky, and the intricate details of nature—reflects His handiwork.
- Acts of kindness and love you've experienced or shared with others.
- The joy and warmth of community and relationships rooted in Christ.
- Moments of worship where you've felt God's presence.

(Pause and reflect: What lovely things in your life remind you of God's goodness?)

Focus on What is Admirable

- The faithfulness of God through all seasons of your life.

- The courage of those who live out their faith boldly and inspire others.

- The quiet sacrifices of people who love and serve selflessly.

- Jesus's admirable example of humility, grace, and obedience to God's will.

(Pause and reflect: How can you embody admirable qualities in your walk with Christ?)

If your focus still seems to be hard to keep centered, allow yourself to go back to Chapter 5 and work on one-second living. Allow yourself the opportunity to have God rewire your mind and keep it focused where He has called you. It's taken me years to learn this, and my prayer is that you get it even one day sooner than me.

CHAPTER 9

Mirror, Mirror

We all know the line, *"Mirror, Mirror on the wall, who's the fairest of them all?"*[13] It's spoken by the villain in the story rather than the hero. When I was a little girl, I loved the image I saw when the mirror was around. What I saw captivated me and, in fact, at times, I was called full of myself. That little version of me saw a story yet to be revealed, and she saw the beauty in me that God wanted me to see. The story was altered. As the years went by, I was told what others saw, and labels began to make their appearance. These labels were dormant seeds, waiting for an event to make them grow. The mirror became an area I avoided, because to look at myself might mean I'd have to see myself, and to see myself might mean that all I would see was all the bad that had been done to me, and all the bad that I then chose to do.

After the trauma of my assault occurred, when I looked in

---

13   *Snow White and the Seven Dwarfs.* Directed by David Hand, Walt Disney Productions, 1937. Distributed by Buena Vista Film Distribution Co., Walt Disney Home Video.

the mirror, I saw everything wrong and nothing right. The villain of what I saw caused me to hide in the darkness and try to mask myself by looking like I was told I should look. The lies planted in the past became the weeds that started to grow, and despising my looks and body became a part of my subconscious. Consciously, I presented myself as a confident young girl, or more so, a woman. I dressed up, I did my makeup, took a lot of selfies, and I searched for a reflection of the world to tell me I was loved and I belonged.

Unfortunately, those messages came from males and came with hidden agendas that were found out during an identity crisis I had after my sexual assault. So, in the mirror I saw the villain, and the mirror became the last place I wanted to look. To make eye contact with that version of myself would have caused a breaking that she could not have endured. So, the mirror was meant to only make sure I looked like the world wanted me to, and that I looked put-together. That version of me could not remember the younger me, and the beauty she chose to behold.

That younger me was hiding, protected from the story. She knew the truth, and she was just waiting for the day that the reflection would be clear so she could be a part of reminding me of who I was.

A LOVED IDENTITY

As a mental health therapist, I have recognized that within the concepts of identity is the need to feel loved in order to know who you are. Unconditional love, which we Christians are encouraged to do, seems so hard to find in its purest form in this world and must come from God.

The fall of 2019 was nine years after my assault. I had been married for about nine months when my dog of eleven years passed away. I was in another identity shift, and due to that, my image was hard to look at. My marriage felt like it was crumbling, and the Enemy was speaking his lies to me again. It had been a long time since I had to work through that version of myself. This was the first time I had to face it within my marriage and without the one thing that had seemed to know me and love me unconditionally. The dog who was with me before the trauma was now gone before a new trauma occurred.

COULD GOD TRULY?

I believed my dog unconditionally loved me, but what about God? Did He really love me? Or Jesus? If He did, why was I ever told *God will forgive you,* as if my worth was conditional? As if my trauma was my fault? So, where do we begin to understand unconditional love, to not only accept it but to express it so that our reflection and our identity can be on a firm foundation?

I truly believed that once you were married, unconditional love would just flow naturally. I only believed it because I was blessed to witness that kind of love, and naïve enough to not have ever known true love until my marriage. At that time, I was learning to navigate marriage, and with that came not only learning to love unconditionally but believing I could also be loved unconditionally.

I lived believing that God loved everyone else unconditionally—but probably not me. And as for people loving me unconditionally? I was sure they didn't either. Most didn't know my story, and if they did, I believed they'd judge me just as they judged others. In therapy, we have a practice called "mirror work," but I knew from my experience of trying to change my inner voice to be more positive toward myself that it did not work. For me, I had to think about things that God says about me. I decided to start doing mirror work again and would utilize the song "Jesus

Loves Me." I remember the first few times feeling kind of silly as I looked at myself, but then came the moment when the walls of my soul came down, and I was broken into the reality that Jesus truly does love me. I started to see myself through His eyes. The image changed—I no longer saw the woman with all her flaws, I saw the daughter of the King. The tears that fell were uncontrollable sobs, not just from the current story but all the stories of the past that started from the age of innocence. My reflection and identity no longer reside in what I see, but I pray God gives me His eyes to not only see myself but to see others around me. To see the hurting and the broken, the hidden and the unknown. Now, the image I want to see is more of a reflection of Jesus. My prayer is that people will forget me and just remember the One who moves through me.

How do we cultivate an image of God so that we die to our selfish desires and God shines through? God gave me a vision of the armor of God and how we are supposed to wear it (as previously discussed in Chapter 2). God started to have me actively look at my armor and give Him the pieces that needed to be restored. He then showed me an image of shining armor, so bright that the Enemy was blinded and could not see me. I was awestruck! I started to think increasingly about the armor and how I am going to mindfully make sure I am a willing vessel who allows Him to pour into me so well that He shines through me in all capacities of my life. I want to reflect Him. No longer a villain or a hero, but a vessel. When I look in the mirror, I want to see Him and not me.

One of my absolute favorite movies is the original *Mulan* cartoon. The song "Reflection" is still a song that emotionally impacts me as I truly feel the words. The lyrics and the sound of that song continue to bring me back to God. My reflection is one I am working on to make sure I do not let any condemnation bring me backwards. At times, my reflection does not mirror that of God's. My humanness comes out. I know that I am not perfect, and only Jesus was. Shame is like a stranger who you know but comes knocking on your door. When shame comes knocking at our door, do we go to God? Or do we run away? For years, I ran, I hid, I played Christian but lived worldly. In this season of my life, when the Enemy comes knocking and all I want to do is escape, I decide to write a little in this book for others to read. To maybe know they are not alone and that we all get to the places and spaces of *nowhere* and just need to breathe to get to our *now here* moments.

Now here moments are what I live for, as they transform the feeling of being '*nowhere*' into a place of presence and purpose that I understand deeply. As I am writing, I see myself in the mirror at the end of my bed and I just took a deep breath in. I recentered my thoughts on God and that deep breath was a relief. I believe my *nowhere* is going to be a part of my life and a part of yours. But one space between the letters, one deep breath, one prayer, and God recenters you to the present moment of knowing where you are, and you are filled with stillness and quiet as He breathes calm upon your soul and gives you the strength to rise.

Before we dive into the practical steps of mirror work, let's reflect on why self-image matters so deeply. We can truly step into a position of godly confidence, for the Bible tells us our confidence is in the Lord. That "Godfidence" is what improves our self-image, our identity, and allows us the ability to not only love the Lord with all our heart, soul, and mind but to love our neighbors as we love ourselves. Here are some questions I want you to explore a little: Why do we seek so much to become who we think the world wants us to be, that our image in God gets left behind? Are you comparing yourself to Christ? Do we reflect Him in all we do and say?

MINDFULNESS PRACTICE: MIRROR WORK

Don't rush through this moment. It might feel awkward or even emotional, but remember—it's part of your journey. If you can't do this for yourself yet, do it for the people who love you.

Step 1: Choose Your Scripture

- Reflect on these two verses and choose one that resonates with you:

1. Psalm 139:13–14

"For you created my inmost being; you knit me together in my mother's womb. I praise you because I am fearfully and wonderfully made; your works are wonderful; I know that full well."

2. Jeremiah 1:5

"Before I formed you in the womb I knew you, before you were born, I set you apart; I appointed you as a prophet to the nations."

Write your chosen verse on an index card and place it on your mirror. Feel free to shorten it. For example, *"I praise You because I am fearfully and wonderfully made."*

Step 2: Engage with the Mirror

1. Find a mirror and stand in front of it.
2. Read your chosen verse aloud.
3. Make eye contact with yourself for **5 minutes**. Breathe deeply:

    Inhale: Take in God's truth and love.

    Exhale: Release doubt and negativity.

    Reflection Prompt: Do you believe it? It's okay if you

don't—yet. This practice may take time. Be patient and trust the process.

Step 3: Connect with Your Child Self

1. Recall the familiar children's song, **"Jesus Loves Me."**

2. If you don't know it, look it up on YouTube. Sing or say these words:

   "Jesus loves me this I know, for the Bible tells me so.
   Little ones to Him belong, they are weak but He is strong.
   Yes, Jesus loves me. Yes, Jesus loves me.
   Yes, Jesus loves me, the Bible tells me so."

3. Breathe deeply again:

   Inhale: Take in God's love and affirmation.

   Exhale: Let go of insecurity and fear.

Reflection Prompt: Do you believe these words? Trust that Jesus does love you, not because anyone else says it, but because He does.

Encouragement to Carry Forward

You are fearfully and wonderfully made. This journey isn't about perfection—it's about recognizing the beauty in each step. Keep seeing yourself as God does: chosen, loved, and whole in His presence.

CHAPTER 10

Guidance

"It is wise to keep in mind that something is always guiding you whether it be wittingly or unwittingly."

Barbara Bradley Hagerty[14]

As a young child, I was more of a follower than a leader, but I always tried to find where I belonged and never truly found that place. I would follow my brothers and their friends, much to their distress, as they are four and six years older than I, and some of the things they said to me, the Enemy likes to still play in my head.

They did not want their little sister with them, so the teasing was reckless. They and their friends were mean, and I still have times where I hear their voices from the past that come over me in overwhelming ways. I truly never felt like I fit in, except sometimes at youth group. I wanted so much to be liked that I became who-ever people wanted me to be or whatever I thought people wanted

---

14 Hagerty, Barbara Bradley. "Prayer May Reshape Your Brain … And Your Reality." *NPR*, 20 May 2009, www.npr.org/templates/story/story.php?storyId=104310443.

NOWHERE (NOW HERE): *From Lost to Found*

me to be. A chameleon. Yet I still tried to be a little unique, so I was not fully following, but not fully myself, and not leading, which is why I love to read books and hide away. Books do not expect anything from you; an author will never know if you have read their words. So, my guides as a girl were two older brothers and their friends, and my friends, who were also trying to find themselves. Right there in the midst was a hidden and hurting me. I was also being led by the voices in my head from the Enemy, the fears, depression, and anxiety.

My parents also guided me, but I was not fully sure what they wanted from me either besides following God. I became a chameleon, and now that is one of my greatest superpowers as a therapist, but back then, it was not helpful in the process of finding who I was.

When you navigate trauma as a young girl, you must become different things to protect yourself. When I was a teenager, I was guided by some friends and a wonderful, amazing youth group leader. If it were not for that youth group, I am not sure I would have survived some of the events of the teen years. Youth groups were such a great outlet for me, and I was able to really create authentic friendships.

I still did not know where I belonged or how to be the pretty girl, so I became what the world would label a tomboy. I am thankful to God that those things occurred in the 90s and not in today's gender confusion.

One of the girls in the youth group was, unfortunately, a bad influence on me. She became a guide in some capacities. I did not want her to be, but she was. She was the one who had me over for a sleepover with the girls who decided to utilize a satanic board game (the story referenced in Chapter 3). That was one of the first times that the voices were no longer in my head, but I was seeing and feeling things that were real in the spiritual realms. I started to pray, and God intervened. Unfortunately, I lived on the side of the fear of spiritualism for so long because of that story instead of remembering how God showed up and showed off in those moments, and how He did it through me. He was able to use a girl in her teen years who did not even know who she was or who was leading her. I could not see that then. I chose to close the door spiritually, not only to the Enemy's spiritual world, but the Holy Spirit's as well.

In my later teens and my first year of college, I was so excited! I was going to a Bible college—I would finally find a space where I belonged, right? Wrong. I now have an even better understanding of the people who leave the faith because of the people who are in the faith. I never felt more condemned and judged than I did at that Bible college. I again was not sure where I belonged, who I was, or who was leading me. I had made a commitment to my parents not to date in the first year, which I am so grateful for.

What I regret is that in telling guys I was not going to date, I became like a target to see if they could convince me to date them. The rumors I heard about myself and the names that I was told I was being called were awful. Whore. Attention seeker. Desperate. Ugly. Etc. These stories were being told to me. Whether those words were ever said by those people, I will never truly know. Nor is knowing important; what is important to note is that the Enemy was able to use more labels upon me. Those labels became a new guide of sorts. I knew I was not a whore, but later that word would haunt me after I was sexually assaulted. I knew I was not trying to date all the guys; I just seemed to get along better with guys. I knew I had never been kissed, but that was not believed. I knew the truths of the story, but I did not know myself, and therefore, the truth did not matter anymore when Satan knocked me down. I recall the guys who told me no one would ever want to be with me if I were a virgin. I was shocked by that at a Bible college, and it was used by the Enemy after the assault. I was constantly being told no man would ever want me if I was unwilling to participate sexually with them. Then, after my sexual assault, the Enemy whispered that no Christian man would ever want me.

Due to the one dating relationship I had at that college and the way I was being treated by him and others, I decided to transfer my classes to online school in the spring semester of my sophomore year. It was so hard to be called all these names that were not my identity or what I was doing, merely because someone else was hurt. He called me all kinds of names after I broke up with him. He was convinced I broke up with him because I wanted to date someone else. His text messages were constant and accusatory. At the time, my friends chose to be his friend over mine. I was lost and alone, broken and hurting, and the stories that were going on were ones I kept mostly to myself. In the brokenness, I went back home. It was another area where I was lost. I continued to pray, to read the Bible, and to seek after Go,d but I still had no clue what was guiding me. I was letting the storms of life move me in whatever direction they wanted me to go.

If I could go back to the younger me and talk to her, I would say, "You are seen, known, loved, and cherished by Someone willing to die for you." Why did those messages not seem to apply to me, but to everyone else? I know why now; I was trying to do it on my own and seeking affirmation from the world. I sought others' love and support and did not seek God's.

The Enemy's voice was louder than my parents', and it was true for me that the negatives were stronger than any positives. I also lived in the darkness of my story, alone, isolated, and ashamed. It was the perfect breeding ground for Satan to start planting and growing seeds of death within me. Those seeds were planted, and the problem was that I watered them, fed them, and let them grow. The traumas were not my choice, but what I did with them afterwards was my choice.

Because I was unaware of how to guide and protect myself, I shut the door to a power that was real. We talked earlier about the Holy Spirit and how the backdraft he has prepared for us can help us. The truth was, I didn't know that then. I didn't know that He was the guide, and the power that I needed to truly know and understand where I was going and where my identity lay.

If we all explore our lives, we can find what guided us in different parts of our stories, whether it be people, circumstances, trauma, or culture. Those guides at the time may have been ways to protect yourself, but there is a God who wants to guide and protect you on a higher level. As I was sitting in prayer the other day, these are the words God brought to me, *"I've brought you out of the darkness to mountains of breath, I will bring you to valleys because I want you wholly refined and purified. Ready for what I am doing. Sit in victory when you need to."* Too often, we slide into the new valley and call it backsliding when God wants to walk with us down the mountain to show us not only the mountain of promise on the other side, but to help us in the valley. For me, I have realized walking with Jesus is literally walking from one mountain top down to a valley, then climbing up the next mountain top. I am grateful that I keep moving, now that I know how to sit at the table in the valley, and how to breathe God's breath to get me to the other side. The valley holds a new beauty for me that I never knew existed. It's a beautiful valley, when we walk like the Psalms tell us to.

As we explore this next mindfulness practice, I want you to prayerfully invite the inner child in yourself to be present and let God become the only Guide that matters and the only voice you want to listen to.

MINDFULNESS PRACTICE: EXPLORING YOUR GUIDE

1. **Settle into Stillness**: Find a quiet place where you won't be interrupted. Take a few deep breaths to calm your mind.

2. **Prayerful Reflection**: Ask God to reveal what has been guiding your life.

3. **Questions for Reflection**:
    *   What or who has been guiding me?
    *   Is it my emotions, my circumstances, my past, or my accomplishments?
    *   Has this guidance brought peace or chaos?

4. **Scriptural Anchor**: Meditate on John 16:13: *"But when he, the Spirit of truth, comes, he will guide you into all the truth..."*.

5. **Journaling**: Write your reflections in a journal. What do you feel God is revealing to you? How can you allow the Holy Spirit to guide you more fully?

6. **Closing Prayer**: Surrender your guidance to God, asking Him to be your ultimate leader and source of peace.

CHAPTER 11

Nowhere Again?

Unfortunately, we can be *nowhere* again. As I shared before, I am back there again while writing this book, and I am scrambling. When I do fall into *nowhere* again, I am able to get out of it much faster with all of the techniques and coping mechanisms I have learned. As we continue our life journeys, we are daily a work in progress. I have come to accept that I can do all the work in the world and think I'm a healed version of myself, only for God to lovingly show me something else that is impacting me. Something else to notice and another area to heal from. Something new could also occur, whether it be a new trauma or a reminder of the traumas of the past that make the current story a little difficult to handle again.

I tell my people that adult me is okay; it is not that version. It is a younger version of me. As I step into this space to put it into words, I believe God wants me to put it out in the world that I get attacked in many capacities, and younger versions of myself remember how those attacks went in the past.

I have just this week started waking up and every day saying, "You are a daughter of God, and Jesus died for all your sins so that you can live free today." It helps for a moment, and then I cry. *Nowhere* is a lot easier to navigate now with the coping strategies and tools that I have learned and have included in this book, so that hopefully it will be easier for you too.

As I am navigating these spaces again, I get a text from my mom. The text says, "I feel like the spirit world is extremely overactive right now, like electricity in the air." I told her it is. In the last few years, *nowhere* has taught me a lot about the spiritual world.

My awareness of God's spiritual world is beautiful. He gives me insights into wars and battles that I am sometimes unaware of, and at other times I am aware of. I know that God told me to write this book. I know that it is meant to be read by you, dear friend who is reading this.

However, it is meant to be read by me, too. As I was in the space of *nowhere* today, I turned on worship music and started to breathe deeply. My two-year-old looked at me and said, "You sad, Mama?" I let him know that God and Mama are working through things and that sometimes Mama must cry. I breathe. I feel. I try not to escape. Then I take my kid to the Wednesday night church event because I do not want to stop life, even if I feel like I am unsure how to do life right now. I just smiled at that sentence and giggled a little. I know a part of me is being a little melodramatic because I have survived all the worst days that I thought I would not survive.

I truly did not think that by writing this book, I would get sent back to the younger versions of me as a child and remember all the struggles again. I know that I have been made whole, but this journey is difficult. To cry, to write, to not write. To give up, push forward, and move on.

As I am writing this chapter, I am in this place. I was not going to write tonight; I was going to succumb to avoidance, which happens to be a very maladaptive coping mechanism of mine.

However, here I am – vulnerably admitting to you, my dear reader, that I can also at times go back to *nowhere* even though I have been on the journey of being present for a long time. I sit here, exhausted. I wonder what God is truly going to do through this book, wonder if He is happy with me, and if I am making a difference in this world that brings people closer to Jesus. Then I am reminded that God is happy with me merely because I am His child. His love is truly unconditional, and there is nothing I can do or not do to make Him love me more or less than He already does. I know that the Enemy wants to take me out, and he wants to take you out, too. What I know even more than that is that God has promised victory and an abundant life. Breathe that knowledge in and let the weight you're carrying that's not meant for you be lifted. Allow yourself to go into the shelter of His wing and just be still.

Be still with me so that we can know that God is God and no matter what we are feeling He has not forsaken us or abandoned us—and He still sits on His throne waiting to call us home. He loves us just because of who we are, and He loves us even when we are struggling.

I recently watched a beautiful fire, and as the smoke was rising, the sunbeams started to play through the trees, and the smoke created a wave of beauty. It was such a beautiful picture to behold, and I am so grateful that I was present and watching the scene play out. I could see that one item by itself held power and beauty, but when the fire became the smoke in the sun's beams, it was breathtaking. I was able to capture the moment in both a photograph and a video. As I was looking at that scene again tonight, it brought me back to the place where I saw it. I was not completely in *nowhere* emotionally at that moment, but feelings of being lost were trying to creep in. It sometimes happens to me when I go back to my family home. God gave me the beautiful moment and gave me more insight into the Trinity at work.

There is power in all three as individuals and also beautiful bold power when we allow Them to work together in us. As I have grown and matured, I no longer see the spiritual realm as scary, but one of power and truth. The Enemy's lies of the spiritual world no longer hold themselves over me, and I love talking about Jesus' victory over Satan and how I no longer fear. In fact, the fear that I do have is the fear of the Lord. The abundant life is ours for the taking, and God wants all of us to have freedom here on earth.

So when you're *nowhere* again, even after you have learned, I want you to remember that I have been there and know I will be there again. Not because I am regressing, but because it is an area where I was protecting myself, an area where I have learned the most about myself, and an area that reminds me to cast my cares upon the Lord and create my *now*-present space.

It is not bad to be *nowhere*, it is bad to stay *nowhere*. I recently read a quote that said, "You don't lack motivation, you lack clarity,"[15] and I think that is what we want to gain before we go to *nowhere* again.

So let's do a mindfulness practice that helps us gain clarity as to why we go to *nowhere*, and what we may benefit from doing to get us closer to our present moment. Remember that clarity comes when we allow God's power to illuminate our lives. The power of the Trinity can remove what was lost.

---

15 Clear, James. *Atomic Habits*. Manjul Publishing House Pvt Ltd, 2020.

MINDFULNESS PRACTICE:
FINDING CLARITY IN *"NOWHERE"*

Sometimes, we find ourselves again in a space that feels like *nowhere*—uncertain, unsettled, or disconnected. Instead of staying stuck, let's explore how to use this space as a stepping stone to the present moment, where God can meet us and bring clarity.

Step 1: Recall Your *"Nowhere"* Moments

Take a moment to reflect on a time when you felt like you were in *"nowhere."* What were you experiencing emotionally, physically, or spiritually during that time?

Step 2: Understand the Purpose of *"Nowhere"*

Ask yourself: *What was I trying to accomplish in that space? Was I protecting myself? Escaping from pain? Searching for peace?* Write these reflections down.

Step 3: Recognize the Mixed Nature of *"Nowhere"*

Consider how *"nowhere"* may have served you in some ways and hindered you in others.

- *How did it feel safe?*
- *When did it feel unsafe or unhelpful?*

Step 4: Create a Path from *"Nowhere"* to *"Now Here"*

Imagine finding yourself in *"nowhere"* again. What steps can you take to move toward being fully present in the moment—your *"now here"*?

- *What truths about God's love and guidance can you anchor yourself in?*

- *What practices, like deep breathing or prayer, help you find clarity and peace?*

Step 5: Rest in God's Presence

Take a deep breath in and slowly release it. As you exhale, picture God lifting the weight off your shoulders. Feel His love surrounding you and His presence guiding you from *"nowhere"* to *"now here."*

Step 6: Celebrate Your Plan

You've just created a personalized roadmap for navigating *"nowhere"* moments. Revisit this practice whenever you need clarity and trust that God is with you every step of the way.

CHAPTER 12

We Can Sit Down

"And God raised us up with Christ and seated us with him in the heavenly realms in Christ Jesus"

Ephesians 2:6

I am one of those people who, even when I am allowed to rest, wonder what I should be doing. A lot of that stems from my *nowhere* places. The chameleon of the little girl who has now developed into a grown woman wonders where I am supposed to be and what I am supposed to be doing. I struggle at times to fully gauge what I "need" in the moment. I know a lot of beneficial things that could help me to cope, and I definitely know my go-to, which is avoidance. Speaking of avoidance, I almost was not going to write right now. Not because I don't want to write, but because it's 10:15 p.m. and I know that sleep would be good, but I also know that television would be a great mind-numbing technique. The reality is the spiritual warfare that is going on in our world currently means that I need to write the words God has given me. So that hopefully, even one person learns how to be where they are and with God. I choose to sit down in victory and start writing the words He has laid on my heart to put in this book for you, my reader. If something in this book truly stands out to you and brings you to a more healed version of yourself, and you wonder how I wrote something that spoke to you so deeply, it is not because of me. It is because God has given me the words that were meant for you, because He wants you to be truly found in Him.

I have read the scripture "And God raised us from the dead along with Christ and seated us with him in the heavenly realms because we are united with Christ Jesus" (Ephesians 2:6, NLT) as many times as I have read the Bible. It was not until it was pointed out that we are *seated* that I truly got to thinking about it. Priscilla Shirer, in her Armor of God study, references that the time people sit down when war is going on is when they have already won. From this scripture, it is important to know that we are seated with God. This means we are in victory, as the Bible tells us.

The biggest thing I have seen within myself and other people is that we are not warring from a place of victory but rather defeat. I used to pray from a stance of "stand up and fight," but also with the fear that God would not hear me, or He would hear me but would not care, and would just do His will anyway. I have struggled with Jesus' words when He was in the Garden of Gethsemane because I understood them to say that Jesus did not want to do what He was being asked to do, and that God did not care. It was not until I studied that scripture more that I realized that Jesus was showing us a vulnerable flesh prayer, and then He went to His spirit, which was willing and said, "But I want Your will to be done." I always heard it or read it as—"Not my will, but Your will be done." When I read it again, I understood the meaning to be more, "Not my will, but I *want* your will to be done." I had a spiritual awakening. I had unintentionally shut God out and only went to Jesus. I felt like I could relate to Jesus because, like Jesus, God also let bad things happen to me. Then Jesus started to draw me near to His Father, and it was in that place that I connected the Trinity all together and had access to a triple power. Yes, They are the three-in-one, and I never doubted that, but I was not accessing Them in the ways that would give me freedom here on earth. I believed in the Trinity, but I was not in relationship with Them.

God was not some mean father who made Jesus. God and Jesus were always one and knew before humans were ever created that Jesus would become like us, so that we could have a relationship with Him. God's heart was broken along with Jesus', but they both wanted a relationship with us, and so they did what only they could do, and that was to restore us to be able to walk with them again in the garden. I want to make sure that whatever is going on in the physical and spiritual worlds, that I first and foremost let God sit on the throne, but also sit with Him in victory's stance, knowing and believing that because of Jesus, we have already won.

Before I sat down for this writing session, my computer drive had lost all these pages. Normally, that would have sent me into a panic. 11,737 words would have been lost. I sat with the Trinity and asked that They restore what was lost, but that if They did not, then I guess I would rewrite those words and pages and maybe it would be better the next time around. This is God's book; He knows what the words need to be, and so I trust. I do not trust my flesh, I do not trust my emotions. I trust that God can help me to sit in victory, to release my flesh to Him, and let Him take all my emotions and make them beautiful.

I pray that you come and join me for the abundant life that God has for us here on earth and sit with us in victory. I pray that this book encourages you to learn what the Bible tells us about

God's will so that you can know when you pray what the Bible says is His will you will know you're praying for His will already.

Now that we have explored an area of sitting, I think it's important that we explore in a deeper way a scripture that I've previously mentioned: "You prepare a table before me in the presence of my enemies" (Psalm 23:5).

I am often walking through different valleys, and I have learned it is a part of the journey of living. There will be highs and lows, there will be triumphs and tribulations. I am learning to rest on the journey, and I invite you to join me. Writing my story has had moments of valleys of sadness, of seeing it all come together from the broken to the brokenly beautiful. I also regularly walk with a lot of different people in the valleys as we navigate getting closer to God through counseling. God has me remind them to sit down at their table, to rest, to trust, and to let the Holy Spirit's fruit be plentiful even in the valley. I also tell them not to let anyone else eat from what God has given to them, like Louie Giglio references in his book *Don't Give the Enemy a Seat at Your Table.*[16] He shares about a time when a stranger sat down and visited with him while he was having dinner with his wife for her birthday. From that story, he realized how often we may be allowing the enemy to sit at the table God has prepared for us.

Susie Larson also discusses in her book *Your Powerful Prayers* how we either choose to sit at the orphan table where the Enemy condemns us or we can sit at the heir table and know that because we are God's children we can sit at that table and He accepts us

16   Giglio, Louie. *Don't Give the Enemy a Seat at Your Table: It's Time to Win The Battle of Your Mind...* Passion Publishing, W Publishing, an Imprint of Thomas Nelson, 2021.

because we are His and because of what Jesus has done for us.[17]

So, from two scripture verses, we are told we get to sit down, and both are in victorious places. One is in the throne room, another is in the valley, and even with enemies around us. We have a table meant for us. I pray that we learn to sit together and to allow God to be God and be still in the shelter of His wings.

---

17 Larson, Susie. *Your Powerful Prayers: Reaching the Heart of God with a Bold and Humble Faith.* Bethany House Publishers, 2016.

MINDFULNESS PRACTICE:
SITTING IN VICTORY

1. Set the Scene

Find a quiet space where you can reflect without distractions. Sit comfortably, close your eyes, and take a deep breath in through your nose. Exhale slowly through your mouth.

2. Reflect on the Valley

- Picture yourself in a valley. Visualize a table set before you, as described in *Psalm 23*.

- Ask yourself:
  Am I sitting at the heir's table or the orphan table?
  Why have I chosen this table?

3. Invite God's Presence

Imagine Jesus sitting beside you at the table. Feel His love and victory surrounding you. Pray: *"Lord, help me rest in Your victory. Teach me to sit with You and trust in Your provision."*

4. Explore Rest

- Reflect on your current approach to rest:
  Do I allow myself to rest in God's presence?
  How do I rest physically, emotionally, and spiritually?

- Ask God to show you new ways to rest and trust Him.

5. Live from Victory

- Visualize yourself seated with Christ in the heavenly realms (*Ephesians 2:6*). Imagine the peace, power, and purpose that flow from this position of victory.

- Reflect:
  How would my life change if I truly lived from a victorious stance?

6. Closing Prayer

- Pray:
  "Lord, thank You for inviting me to sit with You—in the valley, at the table, and in victory. Help me live each day from this place of rest and trust. Amen."

CHAPTER 13

This Seems Upside-Down

"Then he called the crowd to join his disciples and said, 'If any of you wants to be my follower, you must give up your own way, take up your cross, and follow me. If you try to hang on to your life, you will lose it. But if you give up your life for my sake and for the sake of the Good News, you will save it. And what do you benefit if you gain the whole world but lose your own soul? Is anything worth more than your soul? If anyone is ashamed of me and my message in these adulterous and sinful days, the Son of Man will be ashamed of that person when he returns in the glory of his Father with the holy angels.'"

Mark 8:34–38, NLT

The scripture above is teaching us how to live in the world upside-down. So many times, as I counsel people or even do self-work, I have to start thinking upside-down. The Bible tells us that we must give up our own way. I am learning that much of my own way seems to be right side up to the world and seems to make sense to my brain. I must also go to the scripture that reminds me not to lean on my own understanding but, in all my ways, acknowledge Him (Proverbs 3:5–6). So again, it is upside-down living. Many times in life, I must stop trying to control the outcomes and trust the One who controls the world. I must stop leaning on my eyes and start looking at things from a spiritual perspective. When I saw things from my own perspective, it led me to depression, anxiety, angst, and suicidal thoughts. The suicidal thoughts began as a teenager and were woven through my story like a thread connected to a tapestry, which, if pulled, would cause all of me to come undone. I believe the Enemy wants our lives, because each and every one of us is made in God's image, and we are called to a bigger, more purposeful story. The thread had to be pulled; I could no longer live with those thoughts.

In my second year of marriage, those thoughts became more extreme as I was going through some hormonal changes at the time. The suicidal thoughts were more present, and I was prepared and ready. I'm not sure what stopped me from acting, but I recall thinking of all the people I couldn't do that to. My family, my husband, and my clients. So many of them have stayed a little longer to get to the other side, simply because I believed they could. So, I pulled the thread. The tapestry was demolished. It was ruined, no longer even a picture of something tangible, but a mess of thread on the ground. Because when I started to pull one thread of lies out of my life, all the other lies had to come out too.

So I sat in a brokenness that made no sense, that went against the culture I was raised in, which told me to "suck it up and deal with it." I sat in the mess for a while, but it was good. I healed in that mess for a moment. God grabbed the threads from before the lies began and started to make me new. The tapestry started to make sense and flowed together well. The image was a picture I'd never seen, but more beautifully made than the one before. I may have had to get to the end of myself, but at the end of myself was Jesus and He didn't take away who I was or what I'd done, He enhanced who He was and what He had done, and His sacrifice that covered and made atonement for the sins of my story and the stories of others.

There are times I start to notice a new thread trying to come back or be added. I am aware that I will no longer be the one trying to weave the story together, nor will I allow the Enemy to put in his lies anymore. A new thread comes, and I bring it to God and ask Him if it's meant for this tapestry. There are threads that I, in my flesh, did not want, but He said yes to. There are threads in my flesh I did want, and He said no to. All of the threads, when connected to Him, can someday make sense, whether it be here on earth or someday in Heaven.

The threads of my trauma make sense to me now. Why? Because you, my dear reader, need to know that God has a new tapestry for you, and He wants to help you make all things good and remove the lies of the Enemy and your cultural upbringing, the lies of the humans in your story, the abuse, and the trauma. All these things are still a part of my tapestry, but they are woven in truth and no longer hold a negative hold on me. The cultural "suck it up and deal with it" is no longer a negative but a point of resilience. It is also what I must do when I am in professional mode for whatever I am navigating, and now, after that mode is gone, I process and I work through what needs to be worked through. I refuse to let the Enemy have a foothold anymore. He's had too many in my life, so I run to God and stay in the shelter of His wings and His love and His identity.

To allow the Maker of me to be the One who makes my daily story and creates me the way He wants me to be is upside-down living. I don't want to always find joy, I don't want to always be kind, I don't want to always forgive. But in the upside-down living, I have learned I love the consequences of finding joy, I love the consequences of being kind, I love the consequences of forgiving. I love the abundant life living here on this earth, and that is upside-down living. I do not hide away in my struggles anymore, and I run to my prayer warriors and God when the struggles want to overtake me. I let my people have a part in praying and fighting with me, because even Jesus—the most perfect man on earth—did not walk alone.

The biblical stories show us how things don't make sense but always work out for our good and God's glory, and many of the people in the Bible also came out blessed. Peter, one of Jesus' closest disciples, had strong faith and was bold in his declarations. He even promised Jesus that he would never deny Him, even if it cost him his life (Luke 22:33). Yet, when Jesus was arrested, fear took hold of Peter. In a devastating moment, he denied knowing Jesus three times—just as Jesus had predicted. When he realized what he had done, Peter wept bitterly, overcome with shame and failure.

At that moment, it must have felt like everything was falling apart—his courage, his loyalty, and even his identity as a disciple. But Jesus wasn't done with Peter. After the resurrection, Jesus lovingly restored him by asking three times, "Do you love me?" (John 21:15–19). With each response, Peter was given a renewed purpose—to feed and tend to Jesus' sheep.

Peter's story is a powerful example of how even when we feel like we've completely failed or lost our way, God's grace restores and redirects us. What seemed like the end of Peter's calling was actually the beginning of his leadership in the early church. All because Peter chose to believe in the impossible God, who says with Me things are possible (Matthew 19:26).

I remember a long time ago, I saw a post that took the word "Impossible" and changed it to "I'm Possible." I think people use that phrase and then rely on their own strength, but if we break the word down even a little bit more, we see "I Am Possible," and that leads us right back to the Bible. One of God's names is I Am, and so God is Possible, and when we live with Him, when we choose to live upside-down and not be like this world, He makes things possible and makes a way where there seems to be no way.

I continue to live upside-down, and sometimes it makes people frustrated with me. I hear things like "What about discipline, what about rules, what about boundaries?" I teach all of those things and more, but the biggest area I want to teach is upside-down living, which comes with salvation, first and foremost. Then it comes with love, grace, and mercy. My biggest goal for the world is that everyone comes to know Jesus—and that means I have learned how to have forgiveness, how to release what has been done, and how to move into freedom living.

The man who assaulted me has never apologized; he probably would tell the story completely differently. I have forgiven him, not because of anything he has said or done, but because of what Jesus has done.

It was a journey to get there, but I continued to persevere towards it. I would write in my journal, "Jesus, please cover him with your forgiveness and help me to get to where I can forgive." See, to be honest, my flesh was weak, the pain was real, and I wanted so badly for him or others to hurt because I was broken and hurting. My soul was willing, though—my soul was willing to work towards freedom. My soul wanted to be obedient and listen to what God says in the Bible, and truly, truly, truly be like Jesus. I had to live upside-down because the Bible tells me that I must forgive others as Christ has forgiven me. I wanted to be free from the story that was put upon me and step into the story that was meant for me.

Can I be even more real with you? It is hard to live upside-down when a lot of people don't. I believe God has called all Christians to live upside-down because the Bible tells us so, but I look around and I see a lot of comfortable living. Sometimes comfortable in peace, and sometimes comfortable in chaos. I want people to be uncomfortable in a beautiful way.

I would never have gotten to this place had it not been for my story. I am grateful that even when I stopped fighting for freedom, God never stopped seeking after me, and the Holy Spirit never stopped fighting for me. Sometimes I wonder why, but I also know there is power in prayer, and I have had a lot of people praying for me.

Guess what? Those people who prayed for me are joining me in prayer for you. By reading this book so that you can be found, you have stepped into God's covering over me.

I still have to navigate feelings of isolation and loneliness. I am grateful Jesus knows that feeling. Being an introvert who is an empath and has Holy Spirit fire sometimes means I need to be alone to get refreshed. Jesus also needed that. However, it also means that God has called me into positions that He wants me in. He called me to lead a women's small group that He named "W.H.E.W" (Women Helping Encourage Women). Through it, I had to navigate my younger self, and even though I created the group, I wondered if I even belonged. I've also gone through many times where no one showed up. I prayed about potentially stopping, and God told me that even if I am the only one who ever shows up, I will continue to run the group, and He will meet me in that space.

I am so grateful that when I am starting to feel unsure and lost again, and younger versions of me are hurting, He draws me close, wraps His arms around me, and calls me to just breathe with Him. He settles my soul. I show up at every scheduled meeting for my group, prepared to either meet with women and God, or to meet with only God.

I will continue to listen, continue to obey, and continue to step into whatever He tells me, even if it means I will feel insecure, because the Bible tells me that in my weaknesses, He is strong. To write this book, for me, is to be in my weakness. English was always a hard subject for me; I am not sure if it was because of dyslexia, being taught to read by sight and not by phonics, or just my brain always wanting a continuation of run-on sentences.

So, to write feels like I am in my weaknesses, but God wants my words and so He will shine through my weaknesses and allow people to only see Him.

Before I started with the hope*writers coaching and publishing company, God really put upon my heart that I needed to author my book. I told God, "There are a lot of books out there that say what needs to be said." He told me He has given me stories that I am meant to write. About a month or so later, I got an email that said, "Free 5-day training to write your book." I thought, *Perfect! I will do that, and then I can at least get started.*

That opened the doorway to the company and me stepping out with all my insecurities, but with all the faith that God is going to have me do what He has called me to. He continues to make a way in my story where there seems to be no way. I have had to invite all younger versions of me into this story as we navigate being whole with God and bringing the fragmented self to the present so that I can speak to you not only from wholeness but the remembrance of brokenness and loss.

I was never so lost that God could not find me, and for that I will forever be grateful.

I still can navigate *nowhere*, but because God gave me the sight to see the word as *now here*, I have learned to do a lot of grounding techniques. I pray that through this book you learn even just one thing new, but more importantly, you feel found. Before we get to the mindfulness practice, I want you to see some areas where you can choose to live upside-down daily. Living upside-down requires God's strength and guidance, which He promises to provide.

WHAT DAILY UPSIDE-DOWN LIVING CAN LOOK LIKE

- **Wake up feeling rushed** – Choose stillness and pace.

- **Wake up feeling down** – Choose to count your blessings.

- **Feel like everyone always needs you** – Thank God that He can supply all their needs, your needs, and make your cup run over.

- **Family, a friend, a coworker, or a stranger is rude** – Choose kindness and respond well.

- **Forgot your devotions in the morning** – Choose grace and mercy; release expectations. God still loves you.

- **Driving and someone cuts you off** – Take a deep breath, thank God for that driver, and pray for them.

- **Someone does something horribly wrong, and you're justified in your anger** – Choose forgiveness with God.

Living upside-down means surrendering our reactions to God's guidance and choosing His ways over our instincts. It's not always easy, but His strength is made perfect in our weakness. Let these examples inspire you as you step into upside-down living.

MINDFULNESS PRACTICE: HOW TO LIVE UPSIDE-DOWN

Introduction

Living upside-down means embracing God's perspective, which often contradicts worldly norms. Let's take time to align our hearts with His ways.

Step 1: Set Your Intention for Stillness

- Find a quiet space. Close your eyes and take a deep breath. Exhale slowly.

- Pray: *"Lord, help me to see life from Your perspective. Teach me to let go of my way and embrace Yours."*

Step 2: Meditate on Proverbs 3:1–12

- Read the passage aloud slowly. Focus on these key phrases:
  "Trust in the Lord with all your heart and lean not on your own understanding."
  "Submit to him, and he will make your paths straight."

- Reflect: *What areas of my life am I clinging to my own understanding instead of trusting God?*

Step 3: Meditate on Mark 8:34–38

- Read or listen to the passage. Visualize yourself placing your plans, fears, and desires at the foot of the cross.

- Reflect: *What does "taking up my cross" look like in this season of my life?*

Step 4: Surrender Through Prayer

- Pray: *"Jesus, I give up my way for Yours. Teach me to live with love, grace, and mercy, even when it feels upside-down. Help me trust that You will make the impossible possible."*

Step 5: Take One Practical Step

- Identify one area of your life where you can practice up-side-down living this week.
  Example: Offering forgiveness to someone who hasn't apologized or showing grace where it's undeserved.

- Commit to it in prayer and journal about your experience.

Closing Reflection

End with this truth: *"When I live upside-down, I'm living in alignment with God's will, trusting His strength over my own."*

CHAPTER 14

Now Here

Guess what? You finally made it! To a *now here* marker! I'm not sure about you, but even knowing that a chapter has this title brings me more peace than when we started the beginning of the book with the feeling and sense of being *nowhere*. We are no longer lost, we are found. We are no longer bound; we are free. We are no longer any identity that has been put upon us—we are children and heirs of God.

We are where we were always meant to be. Present. Focused. Still. In today and not in yesterdays or tomorrows. This second. This moment. Breathe with me. Breathe in God and breathe out anything that is not of Him. Look up. Stay here. You are beautifully and wonderfully made in God's image.

If you are already walking with God, just look up and let His love for you flow over you. If you are just beginning to see God as someone you want to know, then realize you are right where He wants you. Letting Him love you and letting His face shine upon you. I am still on this journey with you—you do not have to walk this alone. I often ground myself by looking down at my feet and telling myself, *You are here,* and then look up to God, knowing He sees me and is here. I invite younger versions of myself into my adult, wise mind and let them know we are here, and we are safe. I sit, I breathe, and I let God renew my mind and give me a new heart. I now trust God fully and know that He is a loving and good God.

Where I am right now is only pieces of where I want to be, but I know I am right where God wants me. The reason I know that is my posture is set to receive what He tells me and then to do what He tells me. I am not talking geographically, emotionally, spiritually, or physically. I always believe in growth. What I am referring to is that I know I am under the shelter of His wings. I know that I won't always understand why He asks me to do different things, and I know I will still get flustered, but I am in a posture to listen, hear, and obey. That is my *now here* space. It has nothing to do with my titles, status, degree, background, or relationships. It has everything to do with hearing the voice of the Lord and stepping into immediate obedience.

Jesus' prayer in the Garden of Gethsemane has become one of my favorite prayers when I am struggling with the movements being asked of me. His prayer is vulnerable, powerful, authentic, and real. His flesh was weak, but the Spirit within was strong enough to do what needed to be done. Our flesh is weak, but the Spirit (Holy Spirit) within you is strong enough. You no longer have to walk alone or do it on your own. God, Jesus, and the Holy Spirit want to embrace all versions of you and bring them to where you are now and walk together.

Slow down the constant rush of worldly life and start slowly walking with God within your soul's garden. Let your tears be the fertilizer to your soul's garden to bring healing to all versions of yourself, and let God take the yoke off your shoulders and be still in Him. Weed out the garden of death that the Enemy planted lies in, and let the fruit of the Spirit bring life to the dead. Dancing on things of the past is discussed in the song "Goodbye Yesterday" by Elevation Rhythm, that has met me in the darkness of an old life and helped bring me to the new life promised.[18] So goodbye, yesterday, and hello, today. His mercies are new every day, and His grace is sufficient unto you. There is no condemnation for those who are in Christ.

Nowhere to *now here* is probably one of the simplest concepts, and yet the hardest act. I step into *now here* daily so that I can make sure my posture stays in the present moment. I am often doing the practices of one second living (Chapter 5) and God's breath (Chapter 4) to make sure I can stay in the present.

Every day we have a beautiful gift of the day, with His mercies being new every morning. Every day, we either choose to grow, to unwrap the gift of the day and enjoy every moment, or we choose to stay in the past, allowing our old ways to rule us. I am writing this right after Christmas, and I continue to decide that I want Christmas daily. The joy of Jesus' birth, the love, the kindness, the joy. So, I am bringing that attitude with me everywhere I go. I want you to ask yourself a question: Are you living your life, or is your life living you? Are you opening the present of the day, or are you hiding away the newness of today to live in boxes you didn't want from the past? Let's live today.

Let's start living our lives *Now. Here.*

I invite you to join my *Nowhere* Community by going to my website. I want you to know you're not alone, and in the midst of

---

18 Elevation Worship. *Goodbye Yesterday*. Elevation Worship Records, 2023. *Spotify*, https://open.spotify.com/track/yourtrackURL.

nowhere, you're seen and loved. I understand the journey and the struggle that comes with allowing you not only to find yourself, but more importantly, to find God. The child within you is worth rescuing and bringing into today so that you can live a more present life.

They deserve to be seen, known, loved, and found. They deserve freedom from the chains of the past and the beauty of the current moment.

For those of you on this journey, I hope you are now able to at least emotionally feel safer, but maybe there are other things that are impacting you. Please do not hesitate to seek wise, godly counsel. Jesus did not have to walk alone, and neither do you. It is okay to say that you need more help, and that you are in need of advice and support. Go to PsychologyToday.com and click "Find a Therapist" to find a therapist in your area. You can also search for a Christian counselor if that is what you're seeking.

For those of you wondering about your next step, I encourage you to join the *Nowhere* Community. I also encourage you to put your armor on daily and stay present *now here.* Please feel free to follow me on all social media platforms. You do not have to walk alone, and I would love to be able to support you even after this book is finished.

Before we go, let's celebrate together with one more mindfulness practice that helps us Live *Now Here.*

MINDFULNESS PRACTICE:
LIVING NOW. HERE.

1. Find a Quiet Space

Sit comfortably. Take a deep breath in through your nose, and exhale slowly through your mouth. Repeat this a few times to center yourself.

2. Engage Your Senses

Look around and identify:

- **Five things you see**
- **Four things you hear**
- **Three things you touch**
- **Two things you smell**
- **One thing you taste**

Reflect: *"This is where I am. God is here with me."*

3. Speak Truth Over Yourself

Say aloud or in your mind:

- *"God loves me now. Here."*
- *"I am made in His image."*
- *"I am not a mistake."*
- *"He has fought for me, and He will continue to redeem what the Enemy stole."*

4. Rest in His Presence

Close your eyes and imagine God's love surrounding you like a warm embrace. Pray: *"Lord, thank You for loving me exactly as I am.*

Help me to live in the present, trusting Your goodness."

5. Carry the Moment Forward

As you go about your day, pause occasionally to ground yourself by saying:

- *"I am here. God is with me."*

ADDITIONAL SUPPORT AND RESOURCES

Chapter 1 – Self-Care List

- Create a self-care basket for while you read this book
  - o Inside the basket—
  - o Bottle of water
  - o Small comfort snack
  - o Post-it notes
  - o Index Cards
  - o Pens/Highlighters
  - o Journal
  - o Calm-smelling lotion/spray
  - o Favorite scripture/quote written on post-it notes/index cards
  - o Tissue
  - o Timer (or use your phone)
- On an index card, write "Jesus Loves me" and place in the basket to use for grounding
- If you start to sense you're in need of a break from reading, come to this basket
- Put a timer on for 10 minutes
- Invite Jesus in
- Feel what needs to be felt, cry what needs to be cried over, get angry over what you need to be angry over
- When the timer goes off, go to your basket and ground yourself back to the present moment.

Dear Heavenly Father, first and foremost, thank You for who You are and all You've done. You are so worthy of our praise. I thank You for the one reading this book who needs to work through the story of their life. I pray You bring all versions of them to this moment. Bring Your healing power to create a sound mind and restoration of the self to a wholeness only You can do. Meet with them, love them through, and guide them to You. In Your holy and precious name, Amen.

Use this resource throughout the book and throughout your life. I still have a self-care basket; the items have changed as I have changed, but the concept has remained the same.